Lucky Girl

Sharon Hammond McAlister

with Charles B. Hammond, M.D.

authorHOUSE®

AuthorHouse™
1663 Liberty Drive
Bloomington, IN 47403
www.authorhouse.com
Phone: 1-800-839-8640

First published by AuthorHouse   05/05/2011

ISBN: 978-1-4567-5841-7 (e)
ISBN: 978-1-4567-5842-4 (dj)
ISBN: 978-1-4567-5840-0 (sc)

Library of Congress Control Number: 2011907079

Printed in the United States of America

Life is not about waiting for

The storm to pass...

It's about learning to dance

In the rain.

Author Unknown

PREFACE

You may wonder why I am writing the preface for this book. Sharon developed the idea for the book when first diagnosed with breast cancer. She chronicled her course then wrote of the problems her husband developed thereafter. Unfortunately, she had to stop writing after telling the bulk of the tale. Eventually, I decided to try to finish the book, bringing closure to an amazing story of love, loss, recovery and then more of the same. Sharon H. McAlister is the true author of this book; I am merely the person who "finished up". Hers is a far superior prose while mine is written in a "medical factual style". I vote for hers.

The reader may be a bit perplexed in finding a clear path through this book. The two central themes are "grace with adversity" and "coping". Through breast cancer and its several therapies, to David's battle with ALS, and then her own recurrence of the breast cancer and death, David and Sharon provided both. The reader should also be aware of how little time passed between each series of problems as well as how long the total ordeal lasted. This is a story of dealing with many problems. It brings hope for one's future despite issues and losses that may await each of us.

Sharon's mother, my wife, Peggy, has been deeply involved in my part of the book. My total appreciation is to Ms. Patt Dennos who has been my typist, editor and friend throughout the story and preparation of this manuscript. Thanks also to Ms. Carol Cookerly for her special insights. Any errors or inaccuracies belong to me.

Charles B. Hammond, M.D.

PART I

By Sharon Hammond McAlister

Chapter One

From the outside looking in I suppose my life looks a lot like I hit the jackpot – everything seems to come easy, I'm blessed with good fortune and usually land on my feet. And the inside view feels much the same. They call us lucky girls.

Fine and dandy childhood. Great parents who were so present that you sometimes wished for a little more neglect. My dad was a doctor who defied the stereotype of the absent, on-call physician who missed your dance recital, tennis match, always working, blah, blah, blah. He was there. Oh God, was he there. A stay at home mom who literally really was always there. Oh to have been a latchkey kid. What would have been wrong with a little less supervision? A little brother, who, at three years younger, at times adored me, hated me and most of the time was just my cohort in crime.

I always had enough brains to pretty much skate through school without looking like the dorky smart girl, but slick enough to pull out the grades that were expected of me, never having to work too hard. Cool friends that I got in just the right amount of trouble with but didn't push it so far that bail was involved. I was a freaking debutante for crying out loud.

From high school it all just moved right along. Acceptance to the college of choice. No problem. Scholarship. Ding, ding we have a winner. Pledging the sorority I would have died for. Oh yeah. Boyfriends, parties, lifelong friends and fun, fun, fun. Check, check and check again. Life was good.

And then there was my post college plan. Work, play and play some more, marry by thirty and live happily ever after. Just an inordinate amount of ambition wouldn't you say?

I did get fun jobs, assistant PR manager with the opera, a job with a NASCAR video production company (fun guys) and a job in advertising sales with a magazine. Okay, that particular job ended up costing me more than I made since my sales calls typically ended up with me shopping and spending my commission before I actually made a sale. It was a pretty good run.

And at the oh, so perfect age of 28 I met David. In Hilton Head – oh yeah, beach romance. At a party given by mutual friends instead of a bar where I had spent most of my available time searching for the perfect mate. When you meet somebody through mutual friends I think there is some higher sanctioning power that automatically vets the potential boyfriend and okays him. Could it have been any more ridiculously scripted?

But, we did meet and he was so easy. (Not that way.) All the dating of the past decade seemed so hard when measured against the benchmark he set from the beginning. Let Sharon be Sharon seemed to be his philosophy. Wow, there's a novel idea.

I was all set for the games that inevitably seemed to follow when you started dating. Nothing. He called when we got back to Charlotte and we went out the next Friday. And he had the audacity to actually call me the next day and ask me to a cookout with friends the very next night. That usually brought on the "blech" response from me. Too much too soon. But, it seemed like a good idea to say yes at the time and it still does twenty years later.

So without boring you with all the details of our next year, we were married in November – two months before I turned thirty. Yahoo! Deadline met. Lucky me. The wedding was fabulous, and fun. Do you seem to sense a running thread of fun? Oh yeah, I always have been and still am a big fan of fun.

So we embarked on our new life, moving from Charlotte, on to Atlanta, and finally settling in Greenville, South Carolina where we bought our first house. Which again, just illustrates the luck I seemed to carry with me.

We were driving around neighborhoods trying to decide exactly where we wanted to live. Of course we were both all about living near Greenville Country Club. (I know I'm really starting to sound obnoxious and shallow, but please bear with me.) So, we're driving through this neighborhood and I told David, "This is the street I want to live on."

There wasn't even a house for sale, but I just had the feeling that was where I wanted to live.

So we contacted a realtor a few weeks later and we met her to look at some houses. Yeah, you probably know where this is going. A house had just gone on the market on <u>that</u> street – Brookside Way. Could the street name be even more perfect? Ugh. We saw it, we loved it, we bought it. And for the next ten or twelve years all was good.

We had both decided early on – even before we married – that we didn't want to have children. Totally mutual decision. We just weren't the type we thought. So we lived it up. Pretty much doing whatever we felt like when we felt like it. We had great families and great friends, and there just wasn't a lot of trauma and drama in our lives. Lucky us.

Now, I've intentionally scooted through four decades of my past on a very superficial level because that's not this story. I just needed you to know what and where I came from to put this all in context. This story started a couple of weeks before Christmas in 2002.

I will never forget the actual date, because that's when life, as I knew it, changed irrevocably. December 16, 2002. Just taking a shower, getting ready for the day and I found the lump. Yeah, that kind of lump. The only way to describe the feeling of finding something like that is breath sucking, gut punched terror. I jumped out, got dressed and flew downstairs to David. Surely, this couldn't be happening to me.

Of course David assured me that I was overreacting, since I do have a flair for the dramatic. But of course, somewhere deep inside me I knew this wasn't good, this wasn't good at all.

My doctor saw me that afternoon and immediately got me in to see the radiologist for a mammogram. Oh God, oh God when they move you through that quickly things can't be looking very positive.

So I get the mammogram and I sit there in silent dread and shock, thinking, hey you're the lucky girl. This crap doesn't happen to you. The sickest I'd ever been was with mono in high school (and that comes with a sort of badge of honor). It's got to be some cyst or something. I mean my goodness, it had only been about six months since I'd seen my gynecologist and had a full exam and she hadn't felt a thing.

When the radiologist came in to share the results she pretty much threw my film at me (no eye contact, she must have missed the bedside manner class in med school) and said, "You need to see a surgeon immediately." And she literally left me in the room by myself. Bitch was what I was thinking only to avoid thinking about the reality of my situation. Try getting yourself dressed and driving yourself home with that news. I literally couldn't breathe. But I did get home and the next part of the journey started.

I have to preface the rest of the story by saying that this is NOT a story about a warrior cancer survivor. I hate that stuff. Everybody on this planet has been touched by cancer in one way or another. It's not a why me thing, it's a why <u>not</u> me thing. Cancer is something that happened to me – like a really long bout with the flu. It doesn't define who I am. I don't wear pink ribbons; I don't walk to raise money. I'm done. I've given cancer all I'm going to. (Although I will cop to using those return address labels the various groups send that have the pink ribbons – and I don't send money!)

What I was about to find out was that cancer was the easy part. But, you'll have to go through it with me to see that luck comes in all shapes and sizes. It's often packaged in ways you wouldn't expect and you have to look way, way past all the things you've taken for granted your entire life to see it. And, Lord knows I had taken a lot of things for granted.

So my universe had been forever reordered. That's not necessarily a bad thing. I could never have gotten to the place I am today without my cancer experience. And you'll see that it isn't the worst thing that can happen; in fact I have always said that more good has come out of the situation than bad.

Chapter Two

So I've told what this story is <u>not</u> about; now I'll give you some idea of what it <u>is</u> about. It's about choices. And I was getting ready to make what I thought at the time was the mother of all choices.

I'd just been told I needed to see a surgeon immediately. Well why don't I just whip out my handy book of surgeons and give one a holler?

"Hi Dr. Surgeon, apparently I've got this big honkin' thing in my boob that's scaring the crap out of everybody. You think you could work me in?"

What actually happened is that my ob-gyn called me after talking with the radiologist. Isn't that sweet that she found the time and spine to talk to *her* when she couldn't even give me the time of day. Whatever. Anyway, my doctor suggested a surgeon that she thought I would like. WHAT???? I couldn't give a hoot if I like her, I just don't want her to kill me. She gave me the number and said she would pave the way for me to give Dr. Klove a call.

By now it's Friday, so when I called of course the soonest appointment I could get was on Monday, December 23rd. Merry effing Christmas. Yippee, I get to spend an entire weekend pondering the future of my breasts or the lack thereof. Boy, I bet I was good company.

Monday came and David and I set off to find out what our future would be. And I do include him in that because as anyone who has been grazed, pummeled or mowed down by cancer knows, there's a trickle down effect. Contrary to popular belief (mine that is) it wasn't just all about me.

We had no idea what to expect. I must let you know from the start that

David has an irrational abhorrence to anything medical so I was leading him into the jaws of hell. I really didn't care.

They called my name and the nurse encouraged David to come back with me. I felt like I was pulling a puppy into the pound.

"Man up dude, this is probably the easy part."

No, I didn't say it out loud.

Dr. Klove was indeed quite likeable, under the circumstances that is. She explained that she was going to perform a needle biopsy and it was fine for David to stay. Yeah, right. He opted out. Can't say I blame him, I was ready to opt out myself.

So she starts whipping out needles.

"Just going to put some local anesthesia in here."

Okay, that sounds like a dandy idea. Then she pulled out what, to me, looked like a car's exhaust pipe attached to a syringe. Maybe I should think about closing my eyes now. Better late than never. I really didn't feel much of anything except a tugging as she sucked out a couple of plugs of "the thing."

She bandaged me up and said I could get dressed and she would go get David. While I was dressing she was looking at the plugs under a microscope and getting them ready to go to the lab. This would be a great time for her to say, "Oh, what good news, this doesn't look bad at all."

Nope. Not a word.

So she leaves to get David and she's gone, and gone and still gone. When they finally come back I'm like "what's up with this?" Apparently she had to go find David in the parking lot. I really wasn't exaggerating when I said he detested any and all things medical. But he really was trying.

She sat down in front of us and said, "I'm going to send this to the lab and put a rush on it if that's okay with you."

Uh, yeah, there's an idea.

"But I can tell you from my preliminary opinion you're going to need a mastectomy."

Honestly, I can't tell you I was stunned or even really surprised. This process was moving like an out of control train and at this point I was pretty much just along for the ride.

She went on to explain that I had a couple of options. She said that one option was to have the mastectomy and that they could pull fat from my belly to reconstruct the breast. Now I'm really not kidding when I say that I got giddy with delight at that idea.

"Are you telling me I could get a new boob and a tummy tuck in one fell swoop?"

I was actually laughing, which I think they both interpreted as hysteria. But I wasn't kidding. Damn, I ought to get something out of it. But no.

"I'm afraid you're too thin for that to be effective."

Of all the freaking times in my life for somebody to tell me I'm too thin. Believe me when I say that hasn't been a common theme in my life.

"Another option is for me to perform the mastectomy and then have a plastic surgeon immediately follow me with the reconstruction," she said.

Okay now that doesn't sound like a bad idea. One stop shopping if you will. Go in with boobs and come out with them. The third option was to have the mastectomy and then have reconstruction later. Not a chance.

The fact is that what was scaring me the most was surgery. I told you I've never been sick and the only surgery I had ever had was a tonsillectomy when I was a kid and I don't really even remember that. So one time under the knife, or knives in this case, sounded like my best choice.

I have to sort of stop here for a moment and explain that I wasn't going through this process in a vacuum. Of course when all this started I called my parents. I mentioned that my dad was a doctor. What I didn't mention was that he's an insanely famous doctor. Not my opinion, just a fact. Chairman Emeritus of Obstetrics and Gynecology at Duke University. Google him. Dr. Charles B. Hammond – Duke University. 431,000 hits. Mom, not so famous, but a calm voice in this crazy storm.

The reason that I mention that my dad is well known in medicine is that if I learned one thing through this whole ordeal it was that when it comes to a serious illness, it isn't what you know, it's who you know. And knowing somebody that can move mountains to get info, answers and attention is a pretty good card to have up your sleeve.

After hearing Dr. Klove's opinion that I needed surgery pronto, my first reaction was to have her call my dad. So I dropped his name like a cement block. It had the intended impact. Who needs me to be in the middle translating? I mean really, wouldn't he be in a better position to help me figure this out if he talked to her directly. And God love her, she gave me her cell phone number. In case you don't know, most doctors wouldn't give a patient that kind of access. I told you she was likeable.

She also asked me if I knew an oncologist that I wanted involved in my case. Oddly, I did. And quite well at that. Dr. Giguere was a family friend who went way back. The specifics aren't important. Suffice it to say that there was a pretty strong tie there.

"Oh good, I know Jeff and he's a good choice," she said.

Okey, dokey, I've got a starting point. Great seeing you. So onward and upward -- boy this Christmas was shaping up to be oh so festive.

Chapter Three

David and I are a tad shell shocked to say the least, although I was weirdly calm. I really should have been more freaked out by this time. Have you seen those Japanese prank shows on the Internet where a guy is walking down the street all by himself? He turns a corner and suddenly out of nowhere there are like 150 people running straight for him. All he can do is turn around, try to stay out of the way and run for his life. That is sort of what this whole thing felt like – there just wasn't any time to do anything but keep moving and try to stay out of my own way.

When we got home I did call my parents and gave Dad Dr. Klove's number. I think he still needed professional confirmation of the facts. Meanwhile, a friend of mine (not an incredibly close friend, but someone that I really liked and whose opinion I respected) kept crossing my mind. She lives in Atlanta and maybe a year or so before had found a lump in her breast. At the time I thought her story was sort of crazy and remarkable because while her doctor had recommended a lumpectomy she opted to have a double mastectomy. She had crazy cancer running through her family and didn't want to take a single chance of doing this again. So I called her. Thank God she was home.

"Hi Stacia, know we haven't talked in like three years, but I seem to have a little problem. I've just been told I've got breast cancer and need a mastectomy. If you've got a minute could you take me through your thinking on the decision to have a bilateral mastectomy?"

The *Reader's Digest* version of our conversation was that she'd been to this movie once and didn't want to go again. She also pointed out that when you do both, you get reconstruction on both, so that aesthetically and cosmetically you get a matching pair. Now doesn't that just make all the sense in the world? I knew I couldn't go through this process again, not to mention walking around with the ungodly fear of wondering if or when your other boob might be affected. So I made the choice right then and there to "do a double."

If you haven't been through this what you don't know is that one phone call leads to another and then four more. It's endless. But, before I made or took one more call, it seemed kind of appropriate to discuss my decision with David.

"Hon, I think I'm going to get them both done," I said to him.

We were standing in the kitchen and I'll never forget his face. There was no horror nor did he recoil in <u>any</u> way.

He simply said, "Sharon, this is completely your decision and I will support anything you need to do."

And you know, at that moment I really knew that while this was going to be my dog and pony show for the most part, he was going to do the best he could with what he had. That's really all any of us can do. I had no quivers of fear that he would leave me or love me less because I was scarred and different. That in and of itself is a comforting place to be.

So let the phone calls begin. First Dr. Klove called and said she had checked schedules and the surgery could be done on December 31st. Is the timing of this whole thing just freaking unbelievable? I'd heard somewhere (take into account that I'm a little mentally hammered here) that you didn't want to have surgery on a holiday because the staff is pissed they have to be there and they are usually shorthanded. This is the kind of stuff that kicks into your head, which is why I'm eternally grateful for my father's advice.

I told her I was going to talk to Dad and would call her back. When I talked to Dad he told me unequivocally that the surgery needed to be sooner rather than later. Alrighty then, this really is getting to be a big hairy deal. I told him I was going to do both boobs. I so totally expected him to try and talk me out of it, but once again, a member of my family said, "it's your decision and we support you." I told you I hit the jackpot.

When I called Dr. Klove back to say okay, December 31st it is, I also told her I had decided to have both breasts removed. You know how sometimes there are signs that you might have just lucked up and made the right decision?

She said, "That is exactly what I would do."

Well, let the choir of angels sing.

Again, without boring you with all the mundane details of getting ready for the surgery, December 30th came and my parents did too. I can remember sitting at lunch, sort of having this out of body feeling that was bizarre. I think I sort of said something about being really scared of the surgery. Which is weird since the cancer seemed like the logical thing to be terrified of but it apparently had been relegated to second place.

"I'm spending the night with you tomorrow," said Dad.

I don't know why I was, but I was surprised beyond any description. And thank you Dear God, I wasn't afraid anymore. 'Cause let me tell you if Big Chas is in the house you're walking in with big guns. Of course I knew David and Mom would be there during the day, but to know I had somebody there who actually knew what was going on just gave me a peace I needed desperately. No disrespect to them, I just needed someone who could go to bat for me (although I did see my Mom ream her father's doctor a new one once which is another story for another day).

Chapter Four

I t's 5:30 in the morning -- the day of my surgery. I am decidedly NOT a morning person so this day was already starting off on a bad note. I had to be at the hospital by 6:30 so I just needed to get up and have some time to gather my thoughts by myself. You know, it's really stinkin' dark at that time of the morning. Ick, very depressing. This is exactly why I don't think anything is important enough to do before tenish.

David comes down and we're off. Not a lot of conversation in the car. What exactly is there to say? I know I couldn't think of a thing. Mercifully we were only a few minutes from the hospital so the ride was less excruciating than it could have been.

We're checked in. Believe me, even at 6:15 in the morning they're on top of the business side of the whole thing. You may not make it back out the door, but they are going to make sure they have a way to get your money. Somehow that doesn't strike me as very good customer service. I mean really can you imagine walking into a restaurant and giving them your credit card up front. As it turns out your meal sucks. And they take your money anyway. I don't think so.

Whatever. We're sent to the waiting room. I really was getting antsy about now and my attention span with the 4-year-old magazine was like a gnat on crack. Let's get on with this. Now. Be careful what you wish for.

Finally, they send us to a room to start the IVs and all that fun stuff. I undress and get into the gown and sit down on the rolly bed. I swear I'm not making this next part up. The nurse comes in and hands me a marking pen.

"I need you to use this marker to initial the body parts that are being operated on," she said.

There is something fundamentally wrong with being handed a Sharpie to initial your boobs so that they know they're cutting the right thing. I know I wasn't terribly busty, but couldn't they narrow it down by the process of elimination. Talk about your Auld Lang Syne. Of course it crossed my mind to write something smartass on them like "Happy 'effing New Year to you too!" But I didn't. They were going to have a little more control over the situation than I did.

The next thing I know David is kissing me goodbye and they are wheeling me out the door. Hospitals are incredibly creepy at that time of the morning. None of the usual hustle, bustle. Plus they're wheeling you through back corridors to the operating room and when I say it's deathly quiet I'm not kidding. And anything "deathly" at that moment is not the atmosphere you're looking for. And it's just cold as cold can be.

———

So I'm coming out of the anesthesia in the recovery room and damn I'm thirsty, thirsty, thirsty. I think it was about 2:30 in the afternoon and since on most days by that time I've already ingested about a gallon of Diet Coke, I'm not kidding when I say I was thirsty.

"Please somebody get me a coke," I grogged out.

"Oh good you're waking up," I heard from an impossibly cheery voice.

Just for the record, I don't do cheery. Even as gorked out as I was, I knew she was going to be annoying on many levels. I also knew I needed to get out of here pronto because pissing off nurses is not a good idea. How is it possible that I've just undergone more than five hours of surgery and I'm still a pain in the ass?

"When can I go to my room?" I asked.

Just then my plastic surgeon came in and rescued the nurse from me.

"Sharon, you've only been in here just a little while. I'm surprised you're even awake. We'll get you out of here shortly," he said.

I'm sure I was in and out of consciousness, but the next thing I knew I was being rolled into my room. And whoo boy, what a room. It was the mac daddy of hospital rooms. Even as out of it as I was, I could see that. Sitting area with a couch. A lovely basket of treats. As far as hospital rooms go, I was in the Presidential suite. I told you having Dad there moved mountains. And there was my family. Apprehensive, relieved, tired.

At that point I really was coming out of the anesthesia and I DESPERATELY NEEDED A COKE. Geez, would that be so hard? For God's sake this room was so fancy it probably had a mini bar somewhere. Mom came over and started feeding me ice chips. Very sweet and tender, you could tell she just had to do something. And frankly, there just wasn't a lot for anybody to do. Except, GET ME A DAMN COKE.

Finally, somebody did. I can't be held accountable for remembering everything that went on for the next couple of hours. But, I did finally really wake up and it was just Dad and me. It was New Year's Eve and little did he know, but we were going to party hearty.

They brought me a tray for dinner. Blech.

"Thank you so much, but I'm just not feeling like a plate of vomit was what I was in the mood for."

But there was ice cream. Oh yeah, that I could deal with. I've always had the diet of champions and it was refreshing to see that a little surgery didn't screw that up. Coke and ice cream for dinner. My kind of menu.

So Dad and I settled in for the night. For once in my life I had the remote control. Too bad for Dad I wasn't sleepy either. Hell, I was just staying awake to say yes to morphine. There's a reason that's a controlled substance. Yessirree. Morphine is a beautiful thing. I was awake, really not much pain at all.

I dozed off and on, but sometime around 12:30 or so I just kind of really woke up. Now while this room was fancy, schmancy they hadn't perfected the recliner chair for the visitor. So my Dad, who's 6'3" is pretty much working on his contortionist moves. He ain't comfortable. There was some strange talk show on that I just couldn't grasp – the magical morphine you know.

"Give me the remote control now," said irritable Dad. I think his bedside manner was a little frayed by that time. He'd had a long, long day. So I handed it over and I did go to sleep, nice morphine-induced sleep.

What I found out, after the fact, was that whatever channel I had dozed off on involved some guys fondling each other and I think that pretty much shot his night of sleep to hell and back. Dad's very, okay mostly, open-minded, but he does have his limitations and we had reached them. In a big way.

Chapter Five

Good morning heartache, no good morning boob ache. Not horrible, just a definite reminder of yesterday.

"I'm okay, I'm okay, I'm okay," I told myself. Nothing hurt to an extreme. Nobody was in my room either. What was up with that? Oh yeah, Dad had slipped out sometimes earlier to go change and said they'd be back.

Dr. Giguere, my oncologist, walked in and said, "Whoa, who's got the honeymoon suite?"

I told you it was the room to beat all rooms.

"Just checking in. I'll talk to you in a couple of days. But, you're going home in a couple of hours. I'll call you," he said.

I was actually hoping that this was like when you were dating and some guy told you he'd call you and he didn't. That sucked. But, not hearing from Jeff (Dr. Giguere) would have been just fine.

Meanwhile at home, poor, tired Dad was just trying to get into our house. For some reason nobody had thought of giving him a key to the house. So he's knocking at the door and nobody's answering. Nice. So he gets out his cell phone and calls them from the driveway. No answer. Now, I know him pretty well (I am him) and he's probably getting some kind of pissed off. He's tired, cramped up and probably feeling pretty filthy.

Apparently the school of thought inside the house (that would include Mom and David) was that if anybody was calling about me, Dad had it covered because he was at the hospital. (Thanks guys, what if Dad had died?) And apparently they'd gone deaf overnight because they didn't hear him knocking. That defies all logic since we have two Jack Russell Terriers who are comparable to two hand grenades with teeth. This also explains why having Dad at the hospital was a much better idea than having either of them stay.

So poor Dad finally gets them to answer the door. I'm pretty glad I wasn't on the other side of that event. About the same time I call them to tell them they're busting me out. Whoo, hoo! I want nothing but to get in my own, non-buzzing bed.

Yeah, that was problematic. In order to keep patients from doing God knows what the hospital bed would start buzzing every 20 minutes or so. Not only could you hear it, you could feel it. That's probably fine in a Motel 6, but if you're recovering from major surgery, not so good.

Anyway, so I call them and say, "Hey, they're busting me out. Get over here, especially you Mom, cause I can't lift my hands over my head to get dressed and you're on duty."

Could these people have taken any longer to get their asses over there? Meanwhile, I need somebody to take my catheter out and that seems to be something much like launching the space shuttle.

"Hey, want to get dressed and there's this tube thing happening, not to mention the bag thing that seems to be awful full. Got a minute?"

Oddly, I really don't feel bad at all except for a little tiredness. Ya think? So family shows up and still no action on the catheter. Okay, this is cramping my style and apparently my Dad's too.

"Could we get this taken care of immediately," asked Dad. And he did it in the nicest way possible for somebody who had spent New Year's Eve watching fondling guys and his daughter going through something he never anticipated in his wildest dreams.

Mom, meanwhile, was trying to help me get dressed and we were all just sort of fumbling around because you really can't do the dressing thing with a cath in place. Finally, in comes a nurses' assistant with an attitude. Bad idea.

I know it's New Year's Day, but I'm pretty sure that my bad day trumps your bad day. So get over it and get this catheter out of me. Which she did, but not without everybody taking a close look at her name tag. Bitch is going down.

Finally, we're getting in the car. They brought two cars which still cracks me up today. Did somebody not want to be trapped at the hospital in case something went wrong and I didn't get out? Or were they just sick of being together?

Dr. Wallace, my plastic surgeon, had warned me to be careful. This is hilarious.

"Try not to fall on your chest."

Okay, that shouldn't be a problem. I've spent many years trying not to fall down on my chest. Can't say I've always accomplished that, but have always tried. I'm really finding this whole thing very funny. Apparently I'm still a little out of it.

"Be careful with the seatbelt. Don't let it pull your chest," he said.

Okay, David I think the ball is in your court here. If you wreck and the seatbelt smashes my implants, you have only yourself to blame. Right. I'm in some kind of parallel universe where things that should sound rational just sound bizarre to me. Duh. Don't fall on your chest. Exactly when is it a good idea to fall on your chest? Beware of seatbelts. I'm pretty sure that they should have sent me home with the magic morphine. But, no.

Chapter Six

So a couple of days go by and Dr. Giguere calls and wants to come by and talk with us. Mom and Dad were still at our house taking mighty fine care of me. So Jeff and his wife, Nancy came by late afternoon to talk and have a drink with us. Nothing makes bad news better than getting it with a cocktail chaser.

The bottom line was that it was, in fact, rotten news.

"Here's where we are. You have stage three cancer and 19 of 20 lymph nodes came back positive," he said.

What I heard was "wha, wha, wha." White noise. I took one look at Dad's face and knew this wasn't what we wanted to hear.

"I'm going to schedule you for an MRI and some other tests," he continued.

What I heard that time was, "We're going to stick you in a closed up tube for an hour or so and see if you lose your mind."

I couldn't seem to get any grasp on what should be scaring the crap out of me. Stage three cancer that had invaded my lymph nodes or a fairly simple test that I'm pretty sure hadn't actually killed anybody.

"No way am I going in the tube. I'll do the open air one, but I will not go in the tube."

I guess when things look so insanely out of control you'll pick any battle you think you have a skinny chance of winning.

So the onslaught of tests I had to have was scheduled including the open MRI, which was first up. Open MRI is sort of a lie if they're looking at your big ol' head, which was what my test was.

In fact, they put the equivalent of a weird hockey mask, upside down bowl-like thing over your face and head. The top of it is about two millimeters from your face, which effectively defeats the purpose of it being "open." But I got through it fine.

There were PET scans, bone scans and CAT scans. I think the whole point of all this was "let's find out of there's even any point to treating this."

Nobody said this, but I was operating on a need to know basis at this point because it's just too damn much information to process at once.

In fact I got a message after one of the tests from somebody in Dr. Giguere's office.

"Your bone scan came back negative," she said on the message.

Hmmm, is that a good thing or a bad thing? Turned out to be a good thing, but how am I supposed to know that a negative result is a positive result? The whole process is baffling and I had the luxury of incredible access to my doctor, not to mention my father. I do not know how the average person doesn't just feel like blowing their brains out in confusion and frustration.

After a couple of weeks of the endless tests, blood work and on and on, the plan was to start chemo at the end of January. I was going to undergo eight rounds of dose dense chemo every other week. Boy I was excited.

But before I even got started with the chemo I got to learn how to jab a needle in my own leg. I needed to take some drug for like a week after each round of chemo to keep my white blood count up. Lucky Mom drew the short straw on that fun visit.

David had to go out of town for business so Mom came to stay. So we went over to the office. First they give you an orange to practice your phlebotomy skills on. I don't know about you, but my leg is vastly different from an orange. And I'm pretty sure that it doesn't feel pain quite the same way. Now, I'm not really squeamish about needles, but I've got a whole new respect for diabetics.

Mom was a trooper I have to say. She cooked, hung out and was just there for moral support. She was also a big supporter (okay she whipped out the checkbook in a big way) on getting a wig. Since there was no question that I was going to lose my hair, she paid for the best wig ever. I had already ordered it because my thinking was that hey, if I start wearing it before my hair falls out no one will know. Is there something wrong with me? What an idiot.

Anyway, the wig had come in and it was just a little too long and a little too blonde. A little like Daphne on Scooby Doo. I was trying to make it look as much like my own hair as possible. So I took it to my hair stylist and we put that bad boy on and cut it. Then she took it home and put lowlights in it to tone down the color. I picked it up a few days later and took it home. I tried it on and decided it was still too long. So I took it back and asked Kim to cut some more. The following is really true. I am not making it up.

One of the other stylists who worked in the chair next to her and had seen me in there before with it, saw the wig on one of those wig heads and asked what was up with that.

"It's just a little too long," said Kim

"Wow that grew fast," said the other stylist.

Enough said.

Anyway, the point is that Mom and I decided to go out to dinner after the orange extravaganza and I decided to wear the wig. Now take into account I hadn't lost a hair on my head at this point, I just wanted to see if there was any reaction. So we went to this restaurant that David and I went to pretty much every week. The guy that owned it knew us pretty well.

"Great haircut," he said as he walked by our table.

Mom was the happiest person I had ever seen. She was thrilled and I gotta tell you it didn't suck on my end either. I realized that I could get through this just fine because not only was my family rallying the troops, but my hair issues were handled. One down, who knew how many to go.

Chapter Seven

So I was in go mode. All kinds of proactive, let's go get 'em girl attitude. The American Cancer Society has this program called *Look Good-Feel Better*. I'll tell you up front that for many, many people this is probably a fantastic thing.

The idea is that cosmetic companies donate all kinds of products that are then packaged according to whether your skin is light, medium or dark. They give you a box full of blush, mascara and lots of lotions, potions and all kinds of goodies. And it's FREE!

They hold a session that is led by a make-up artist who teaches you new make-up tricks. Did I mention that it's FREE? This just sounded fantastic to me. God, there ought to be some fun involved in all of this.

I signed up for the session even before I started chemo. I was making damn sure I was going to be prepared for everything. And why not, what's the down side of a free make-up lesson not to mention free make-up.

I arrived and there were maybe ten or so of us. I gotta tell you, never before have I met a more miserable group of women in my life. They were horrible. Half of them were obviously in the middle of chemo and were wearing scarves or weird hats. Not a wig in sight. Now I just don't get that. Maybe it's just me, but why not try? Wasn't this thing called *Look Good —Feel Better?*

"Oh Sharon," I said to myself, "give it a chance, maybe they just don't know what to do and that's why they're here."

Never have I been so wrong. A couple of them started talking about their experience with chemo.

"I hate that drug, the red devil. I can taste it, I've never been so sick and they're giving it to me again in two weeks," one girl whined.

I intentionally use the word whine because she was one miserable chick that I'm guessing didn't exactly have the best outlook on life on her best day.

The conversation continued, swirling around me, making me feel as if I were being sucked into their emotional abyss of pain and misery. So far I was the only one looking good, but definitely not feeling better.

The make-up artist, and I use that term very, very loosely, instructed us to start unpacking our kits. At that point I almost laughed out loud. I've never seen such outdated, strange stuff in my life. Awful colors, icky packaging and some stuff I didn't even know what to do with.

My friend Carol and I decided after the fact that, yeah this stuff was "graciously" donated by cosmetic companies (who will remain nameless) but it was either crap that no department store in their right mind would order or just some manufacturing screw-up.

So, I'm still thinking, who knows, I might learn some tricks. I've never been a make-up diva. In fact, probably the opposite. Not terribly adroit with technique or colors or the whole thing. But, I was still game.

So we're applying foundation and the make-up artiste (I've decided to call her the artiste because she was taking herself way, way too seriously.) tells us she's going to teach us how to apply eyebrows for when we lose them.

WHOA! Nobody ever mentioned losing my eyebrows. That's a deal breaker as far as I'm concerned. I really think eyebrows are a necessary accessory on my face. No thanks, I think I'm finished with this cancer thing. It just sounds more and more inconvenient.

Now, I'm not only *not* interested in penciling in fake eyebrows, I'm looking for the nearest escape. And I mean NOW! We've been here about 30 minutes and the session is supposed to last two hours. There is NO WAY I have another hour and a half of this shit left in me. So I just pipe up and tell the artiste, "Oh my goodness, I must have misread how long this class lasts. I'm going to have to leave to pick up my children. I hate it, you're so awesome and this has been so helpful. Thanks so much."

Yes, I told her I had to pick up my children. Thank God I didn't ever aspire to have children, because I think I just sacrificed them on the altar of the make-up gods. I almost ran out of the room, and yes, I did take the crappy make-up with me. Did I mention that it was FREE?

During this time leading up to chemo, my parents had introduced me, via e-mail, to their good friend also named Peggy. She had gone through virtually the same experience at a very young age too. And man, oh man was she the best friend a cancer chick could have. Like my Mom said, "I can see how people fall in love over the internet, because the friendship you and Peggy have developed is just incredible."

No bullshit from her ever, she just told me what was what, on my terms. Never too much information, just a good human laboratory rat that had gone through it and was always there to answer strange questions or lend an ear, shoulder or whatever I needed.

When I told her about my *Look Good* experience she pretty much busted out laughing. She knew I was going, but had the grace not to prejudice me in advance. She fessed up that the one she had gone to was equally awful. Which made me feel better, because even though I had decided that I was going to be different than that group of depressed dames, her confirmation that there was a different path was so reassuring.

In retrospect that class was probably one of the best things I could have done. Did I want to be one of those women? Did I want to drag every other human in my life into my trauma and drama? Not a stinkin' chance. That was NOT going to be me. Never has anything been more crystal clear in my life. I had choices (and an awesome wig). Whine and bitch, or suck it up and take it as it comes. It really became very simple to me and I knew that I really had learned something at the *Look Good-Feel Better* class.

Chapter Eight

So off we go to chemo. Nothing like a control freak to tell the team that chemo would work for me on Fridays about 10ish. Who knew? They bought it. The actuality of it was that I thought that if I was going to be puking my guts out, David had to work and if he had to deal with sick Sharon, the weekend would be easier.

They had given me a tour of the chemo area. There were some private rooms with grooving recliners with TVs in the room. Oh yeah, bring on The View. Or, there was what I called, the Kum Ba Yah Chemo circle. What a bad idea. Do I really want to sit in a circle with a bunch of sick people and avoid eye contact for four hours? Not a chance.

So in my self-entitled way I told my chemo nurse that I thought I would be much more comfortable in one of those private rooms. God, what an ass. But, yet again, they bought it. Who am I to argue?

First chemo day. I was pretty much panicked. Not that anybody would have known it. I have an amazing capacity to internalize any uncertainty, make a joke, put everyone else at ease, generally just bluff my way through whatever is freaking me out. Not always the best plan.

I was so sure that I was going to just be sick as a dog that I had a spare trash can (with appropriately fitting bags) in the car, a bag full of my friend Peggy's nausea fighting cures and every Diana Krall CD ever recorded. I looked like I was going to spend a day at the freaking beach, minus the beach towel and suntan lotion.

My chemo nurse came in to start the IV. Naively, I just wasn't scared. I mean what's the worst that could happen. I am a dumbass sometimes. I had adamantly fought against having a port put in. I didn't want some weird thing hanging out of my chest. Again, was I fighting the wrong battles?? Idiot. So she's working on finding a vein in my hand and tells me, "You have really skinny, rolling veins. I think we can do this today, but you're going to have to get a port because as we go on I'm afraid we'll blow out your vein."

Again, that stupid skinny thing when it doesn't count for anything that really matters. Can't get a tummy tuck, have to get a port. Screw all of you. But she did get me hooked up and off we went.

Four hours. Have I mentioned that I have the attention span of a really manic two-year-old kid? Thirty minutes into it I was booooorrrrrreeeeed. So I turned on the TV and fidgeted around for the rest of the time.

Okay, so we're done. David is there to pick me up and I'm just waiting, waiting, waiting for the puking to kick in. So far, so good. We get home and he's looking at me like, "When does the puking start?"

Don't know, don't care. All I really want is Chinese food and a glass of wine. Which is so strange, since I could take or leave Chinese food on any normal day. The wine stuff, not so strange, it's good for the soul. But good gracious, Chinese sounds better than anything I can think of. David is looking at me like I've lost my mind and God knows I can't blame him because I'm sort of having an out of body experience myself.

"I know, I usually fight you on the Chinese food thing, but I'm craving Chicken and Cashews. Make it happen," I pretty much ordered him.

David was just happy that things were pretty normal. Me too! About that time, Dr. Gigure called to check on me.

"How are you?"

"Fine. David's getting Chinese for dinner," I answered. (Quite proudly I must admit since I had had visions of my head in a toilet at this point.)

"Be careful, you don't know when it might kick in," he said.

Piss on you and your bad attitude was what went through my mind. Bad Sharon, bad Sharon. He only has your best interests in mind. I only had Chinese on my mind.

Drugs are good. Wow, what a strange segue. But relevant. Dad had a good friend who was an oncology nurse at Duke, Lyn Filip, and she had sent me some very powerful anti-nausea drugs. I was a fan! I took them with all kinds of confidence. I'm a big fan of stuff that prevents stuff like throwing up. I'm not sure if it was just a placebo effect, real drug effect or mind over matter, but I was *never* sick one day during chemo. Lucky girl.

I cruised through the first weekend with trepidation wondering if at any moment the whole thing would fall apart. But no, I was kind of tired but fine.

"This can't be happening for real," I told myself. "You're supposed to be sick and tired and all kinds of screwed up."

Everybody was shocked that I wasn't curled up in a ball in my bathroom. I'm not sure that I was as shocked as everybody else. I think I had, for most of my life, been underestimated. Lucky girl, she's got it going on. Whatever. I really hadn't ever been tested. And nobody, and I mean nobody, really had any confidence that I had the wherewithal to step up and deal.

Guess what? I did. And good for me. Shock was the reaction I got all the way around. Nobody saw this version of Sharon coming. And you know what? HA! That's the best part. They didn't have any idea of what kind of person I had the capacity to be. Apparently my Aunt Judy did. When my Mom expressed her surprise at my strength Judy said, "She's always had that strength, she's just never had to use it."

God Bless you Judy. Why is it that you have to hear it from somebody else to reinforce what you think you know?

Chapter Nine

So I got through the first treatment and really all was well. As well as things can be with Stage 3 cancer that's invaded your lymph nodes. But, I was going to have to get the stinkin' port put in. My chemo nurse had told me about what they call a pass port. No, not a ticket out of this crap, but a port that was implanted in your inner arm, right above the elbow. That sounded like something I could live with.

So the scheduler from the cancer center called me to let me know that I should be at Greenville Memorial at 7:00 am and that somebody should drive me because I would be under "light" sedation. Fabulous.

Only problem was David was in Illinois and the stupid scheduler had told me earlier in the week that I could drive myself. This was becoming problematic. I really had nobody to call. I had a group of friends that I'd hung out with, mostly people that I had worked with, but one of the bitches had decided for some unknown reason that I wasn't worthy and they basically all ditched me.

So here I sit. I called David in tears.

"You have got to get back here. I've got to get this stupid port put in and I can't drive myself, contrary to previous information," I pretty much begged.

"I'll get out of here and get back, may be late tomorrow, but I'll be there," he said.

He did get back and got me where I was supposed to be on time. So there I was in another waiting room. Before he left I gave him strict instructions to please show up when I was done with a cheeseburger from McDonalds and a very, very large Coke. God knows, my appetite wasn't suffering.

So there I was, once again at the freaking crack of dawn waiting for something to happen. They started me in this weird room where there were a bunch of beds that were curtained off from each other. Basically a holding pen for freaky procedures.

After just a little while, I had changed into a gown and a nurse came and took me to another waiting area, which could also be called a bench in a hall. A public, open hall. Freaky. This was getting stranger by the minute.

After a while a guy in scrubs (I pretty much assumed that he was the doctor, but he could have been a janitor) came and called my name and then proceeded to try and talk me out of getting the pass port in my arm and getting one in my chest. I found out after the fact that the chest port takes about a nanosecond to put in and the pass port is somewhat trickier since they have to thread it through a vein in your arm to your heart. If I had actually known all the facts, my vanity involving a scar on my chest might have given way to the quick and efficient alternative.

But I stood my ground by damn, and today I sport a dandy scar just above my elbow which shows every time I wear short sleeves, versus a scar on my chest which would virtually never be seen since I'm not wearing all kinds of chest baring, strapless gowns on a regular basis, or ever. I told you I just hadn't figured out what battles to pick.

So they finally get me on a gurney and wheel me into the room for the procedure at which point there are like three guys in there scurrying around. The doctor draped my arm so that I can't see anything and told me he was going to give me a shot of local anesthesia. At the same time a nurse came in and mentioned, "Whoops, we forgot to start her IV antibiotic and Valium. I'll just get that going now."

Are you kidding me? I'm about one step from getting myself off the table and getting the hell out of there. But wait, it only got weirder.

Now I don't know if any of you remember the very, very bizarre Michael Jackson special where he was sitting in a tree and just being all kinds of Wacko Jacko weirdo. It was at the time when he was accused for the umpteenth time of screwing around with little boys.

So I'm fully, and I do mean FULLY awake and there's my arm behind a drape and the doctor and apparently some newbie in training getting ready to stick some tube in my arm. There was also an aide of some kind sort of hanging around and he says, "Hey did you guys see that Michael Jackson thing on TV last night?

"Uh, yeah I did," I found myself answering.

"Okay, now we're going to make a small incision and start threading the port," came the doctor's voice from the other side.

"Whoa, is he some kind of screwed up or what?" said the aide guy.

"Uh, yeah, ya think," I said.

Now I'm obviously not some kind of prissy prude or something, but is this really actually appropriate conversation in this situation? After a while I heard, "Okay, now I think what I'll do is try this new liquid adhesive instead of stitches. Why don't you try it," said the doctor, apparently to the newbie, or maybe some other random person who might have wandered in.

"Better yet, why don't you do it yourself asshole. I'm not a lab rat," I said to myself.

"I mean what kind of nut climbs up in a tree and acts like that's normal?" said aide boy.

"Um, the whole point of getting this in my arm is to have the least obvious scar. Is this adhesive stuff going to work?" I asked.

I was starting to feel like I was talking to Oz behind the curtain.

"Oh yeah, this will be fine," he said.

I know this wasn't major surgery or anything, but the scheduler said I'd be under light sedation and I'm carrying on dual conversations with at least three people about two entirely different subjects. This can't be normal, can it?

"I mean really could this dude be any weirder?"

Okay, now I'm getting confused. I think the light sedation finally kicked in.

Chapter Ten

So I'm cruising through chemo. I'm astonished that I'm not sick. I am, however, losing my hair at an astonishing rate. But, that's okay, 'cause I've got the kickin' wig going on. But then my eyebrows started to go, and then my eyelashes. Wow, you just don't know how much work your eyelashes do until they're gone.

We're now into probably mid-April and the pollen is at an all time high. The other hair that goes is those very important nose hairs. For every woman who curses nose hairs, say you're sorry and thank God for them. Because without them you are pretty much mainlining snorts of pollen up your nose at an alarming rate.

So I'm a snorting, stuffed up hairless mess of a person. And David is in pretty much the same condition. He's congested, miserable and his voice sounds like he's been on a bender for about two weeks. Needless to say, I'm less than sympathetic at his plight.

"For God's sake, just go to a doctor," I said. "I mean Jeez, I'm getting injected with all this toxic crap and you're sneezing and stuffed up."

Pardon me for not being more sympathetic.

Knowing his hatred of all things medical, this getting an appointment thing is not something that happened immediately. He hemmed and hawed and screwed around until my patience was just shot.

"Listen jerk, I'm in the middle of chemo and I'm sick of your whining about some stinking allergy. Deal with it."

He actually stepped up and got an appointment with an allergy specialist.

The first thing they did was that allergy test that pokes you all over your back and leaves you with all these red spots on you, so you look like you have the measles. Man, he was allergic to pretty much everything. He was a mess and it itched. Again, me, not so sympathetic.

So he's got all kinds of fabulous drugs and we're both seemingly making progress. Except I'm missing my eyelashes a lot. You just don't realize how weird you look without eyebrows and eyelashes.

I called my friend Gwen who did my nails. Nail technicians, much like bartenders, hear it all and she'd become my friend like no other. There's something very intimate about holding hands with a stranger that makes conversation easier. Your guard is down and it's just easy to let it all out.

Gwen was also an aesthetician, which is a fancy description for "beauty school graduate" and had all kinds of experience with makeup and all the stuff that I didn't know jack about, facials, dermabrasion, whatever. I'm such a goob about that stuff.

So she says she's going to put fake eyelashes on me and nobody will know the difference. Well, we move along through that and I look in the mirror and damn I look pretty much normal. Yahoo!

I go home feeling sort of like a normal person. I've got eyelashes! Wow, that feeling lasted for as long as it took to get out of my car and into the house.

"What do you think" I asked David.

He looked at me kind of strangely like I was joking around so I walked into the bathroom to take a look.

Well, apparently the adhesive didn't really take so by the time I was looking at myself, I looked like I had two spiders on my face. The top lashes were kind of hanging off at a weird angle and the bottom ones were sort of hanging down period. At that moment I just had to burst out laughing.

I'd just paid some ridiculous amount of money to get fake eyelashes and what I end up with is worse than no eyelashes at all. I think David was afraid that the spiders were going to send me over the edge so the relief on his face was obvious.

He turned around and walked out of the kitchen into the storage room and came back with his box of fly fishing lures. You know all those fancy feathered, hand-tied special looking lures.

"Maybe some of these will work with a little super glue," he grinned.

"Funny," I answered.

And it was.

I finally finshed chemo at the end of May. Now that was a day to celebrate. Or would have been if I'd had the energy. But, the emotional high was worth it all by itself. I had made it through eight rotten treatments over sixteen weeks and I was really none the worse for wear.

But, weirdly, David was still struggling with all his allergy stuff and was really frustrated. His congestion would seem to clear up and he would feel fine and then the whole thing would flare up again. He was going back and forth to the allergist trying all kinds of different meds which would seem to work and then stop. I was starting to feel sorry for him. It was like he'd had a rotten cold for two or three months.

I was pretty happy that I was going to have a whole month off before I started radiation at the beginning of July. Radiation -- oh boy, seven weeks of fun to look forward to.

That month flew by. My hair actually started to poke out a little. Nothing to brag about, but you should know that when you lose your hair, the first hair that comes back is eyelashes and eyebrows. Hallelujah!

I also gotta tell you that wearing a wig in the South in the summer ain't no picnic. And for some reason the two places I always seemed to go, the cancer center and the grocery store, always had gale force winds all day, every day.

Do you know how weird you look holding the top of your head as you walk through a parking lot? Who cares, I was halfway through this extravaganza of fun and my vanity had taken a back seat. Finally. Too bad that couldn't have happened sooner. I might not have a stinking scar on my arm.

Chapter Eleven

Before I knew it radiation time was here. Oh goody. One thing I hate is to feel overscheduled. Radiation is nothing but being overscheduled. Every day, Monday through Friday, rain or shine. Sounds sort of like a job doesn't it? And since I'd been working for myself for about three years on my <u>own</u> schedule, I wasn't exactly giddy about the prospect of *having* to be somewhere at the same time each and every day.

Before you start radiation they have to go through this process of marking what they call your fields. Since I was still operating on a need to know basis, I hinted around to my friend Peggy that I wasn't sure what to expect.

As always, she was great. She said in her case they just took some films of her chest and then gave her a small dot of a tattoo where to aim the radiation. That didn't sound too bad.

But, no. As always it seemed, and still does, that I can't ever do anything the easy way. Because my tumor had been so extensive and had spread to my lymph nodes I was going to have to have like three or maybe even four areas irradiated. More is not better in the case of radiation.

So I went in the week before I was to start and they took x-rays on some strange machine. Nothing to it, I think. Then came the day of my first treatment. Once again, I got my 10:30 in the morning time slot. Wow, I'm living large. I'm cool with this.

So I put on the gown and they take me into the radiation room. No, I wasn't going to get the little tattoo. They started marking my chest up like that picture showing the different cuts of beef on a cow. They were using different colored liquid, semi-permanent markers that had that wonderful chemical, get you high smell.

There was a big ol' bright blue rectangle here, an orange square there, yellow box here and black square there. I looked like some Indian warrior ready to go into battle. And it took for freakin' ever. For some silly reason they like to be pretty precise where they shoot the radiation. Go figure. They finally finished and put some clear tape over the markings.

"You can shower, but just try not to scrub these areas," said the technician.

Yeah right, so apparently I wasn't going to have a clean chest or right underarm for about seven weeks. Fine.

I met with the radiation oncologist who maps out the plan and the next day I got started. One of my strong suits is punctuality. It's just been ingrained in me from the time I can remember. And waiting is not one of my best events. I changed into my gown and sat down and was delighted when promptly at 10:30 they called me in.

They put me on the table and got me into position, which believe me, isn't nearly as straightforward as it sounds. They kind of nudged me to one side, moved my arm one way and on it went. I was waiting for somebody to tell me to hold my mouth a certain way to make the magic happen. Then they told me, "Don't move. Cause if you move we have to start over."

Why don't you just ask me to reverse the orbit of the earth right after this? Because when you're in this contorted position the only thing you actually want to do is move the hell out of every muscle in your body. And of course, what happens next is that you start to itch. Doesn't always have to be the same place, but I can guarantee when somebody tells you not to move something is going to itch.

This goes on four different times, but the reality is that it only took about fifteen minutes total. It just seemed like forever.

Not really a big deal I thought after it was all over. I can do this.

———

Since most everybody that is getting radiation goes every day, you see the same people. Some might be at the beginning like I was, or in different stages, but what I can tell you for sure is that everybody is rabidly territorial about their appointment time.

There was this annoying old man that kept showing up early. I knew his appointment time was after mine but he kept showing up hoping they'd bump him up in line. One day he started walking up the hall toward the radiation room hollerin', "Hey girlies, I'm ready for you, are you ready for me?"

I swear to God it took every bit of my self control not to tackle the old fart in a full sprint.

Somebody was looking out for that man that day, because one of the technicians walked him back to the waiting area and told him, "Mr. Hill, your appointment isn't until 10:50 so there's no point in showing up early. We have to take the people in the right order."

God bless you tech girl, you just saved a man's life.

———

Radiation is a tedious non-event. At least for the most part. I conquered the itch and even today, if you told me to be still, something would itch and I can mind over matter make that stinking itch stop like nobody's business.

I guess it was probably about three weeks into the process and I was really starting to look like I had a Ninja sunburn. It didn't hurt, primarily because I didn't have that much feeling in the whole right side of my chest. But the funny part is that I was getting such a high dose of radiation that it was going right through me and I had this perfectly square burn mark on my back. Very strange.

I saw my radiation oncologist at one of my visits and he was like, "Yikes, we're going to have to take a break before you catch on fire."

Did I mention how strange radiation people can be? Not to mention the very, very odd sense of humor. I mean that's exactly what you need to hear when you know you have at least another three or four weeks left.

"Will you make sure my husband gets my ashes," I asked very smart-assedly.

He didn't get it. I wasn't surprised.

So I took a break, which wasn't all bad since my car could pretty much drive me there on auto pilot and I was really ready for a break. And then I went back and I finished. I mean I finished it all. No more chemo, no more contortionist radiation. Just a little random blood work here and there. That sounded just perfect. You know your life has been in the toilet when blood work sounds divine.

Chapter Twelve

I'm done. It felt so fantastic not to have any horrible treatment facing me. I'd crawled through glass and gotten through to the other side with minor scrapes. It's almost fall, the leaves were about to change and life was good. Fires on cool nights. Sweating during the warm dog days of summer. I didn't care, just feeling something that wasn't so frightening was so great. The monster wasn't in front of me anymore.

So what now? When you go through such a life changing event the next step is sort of daunting. Do I pick up where I left off? Do I find something to do that I feel passionate about? What would that be? It's sort of like the whole world is out there and you have a second chance to do it right.

And then there was David. His allergies weren't clearing up. The situation seemed so silly and trivial to me. He's hoarse, congested and just generally out of sorts. But, I guess if you've been dealing with all these symptoms for all these months you want some answers. And David was sick and tired of being sick and tired.

The allergy specialist decided that an MRI would be a good idea. I was so oblivious to what was going on with him that it didn't even register that this might be a big deal. He, like I, opted to have the "open MRI." I warned him. And he didn't want me to go with him.

The results of the MRI showed that his upper palate wasn't responding properly, which is what his allergist had noticed. What the hell does that mean? It all seemed very low key, no big deal. Nobody seemed very uptight about any of this so I took my cues from them.

After getting the results of the MRI, which didn't show any kind of weird sinus tumor or something obvious, the allergist referred him to a neurologist. Okay, *now* this is starting to be sort of scary. Neurology isn't a good referral as far as I was concerned. Neuro is scary and, in my mind at least, something bigger and worse than I had any idea about seemed to be lurking around the corner.

But, I'll admit, I was too scared to ask David what he thought. As I've said, he's not the chattiest guy on his best day and I just wanted normalcy. I wanted my life back before cancer, before weird allergies, before the medical profession had taken over our lives.

I wanted to sit in our kitchen on our silly Williams Sonoma stools at our counter that didn't have a bar or eat-in area, just stools at the edge of the counter. Just sit in our outdated kitchen that served our purpose and make some made-up pasta dish that probably sucked but made us feel like we were cool and chef-like.

I wanted to play with our dogs and have Peggy-dog jump airborne into David's lap with the utmost trust that he would catch her in mid-air – and he would. I wanted him to make a vodka tonic and pour me a glass of wine and feel my hair grow back and just go back to the place that was okay before all this shit rained down on us. It was not to be.

Wow, it's already late September and David's appointment seemed to have snuck up on me, but it was the next day. David had always been somewhat stoic in his demeanor, but this time it was downright freaky. I finally got up the nerve to ask him if he had some idea of what was going on. Never did I see this answer coming.

"I think I have ALS, you know Lou Gehrig's disease," he said so quietly I thought surely I must have misheard him.

"Why on earth would you think that's what's going on?" I asked him, sure he'd just lost his mind and that was the problem, not ALS.

"I just do and I'm going to bed. I can't talk about this right now," he said flatly.

I sat on the couch in a dumbfounded stupor. And that is where I stayed until the next morning. There was not a chance that I could possibly get my mind around the nuclear bomb he had just dropped.

An avid reader of mystery and suspense novels, I was a big fan of the author Joy Fielding. So I had pretty much read all of her books. A few years before any of this had happened I stumbled onto one of her books that was decidedly *not* her typical fare – *The First Time*.

It was about a woman diagnosed with Lou Gehrig's disease, and as much as I fought reading that book at the time, because who really wants to spend frivolous reading time on a subject this horrible, I couldn't put it down. I remember sobbing as I read it and how moved I was by the story.

So I had a crystal clear picture of what a diagnosis of ALS would mean to us. I don't care what the medical profession says ALS stands for, the real meaning of ALS is A Life Smashed.

For the uninitiated, ALS stands for Amyotrophic Lateral Sclerosis. ALS is a disease of the parts of the nervous system that control voluntary muscle movement.

The clinical description of ALS explains that nerve cells that control muscle cells are gradually lost. In most cases, the cause is unknown. As these motor neurons are lost, the muscles they control become weak and then nonfunctional. Eventually, the person with ALS is paralyzed.

Death, usually from respiratory complications, typically comes between three and five years after diagnosis (some studies say after symptoms are noted, so the timing is unclear). It could actually be between one and three years. About 10 percent of those with the disease live more than 10 years, and some survive for decades.

But the shit kicker of this stinking disease is that the vast majority of patients retain all brain function and awareness. Ain't that grand? So you're sitting there not able to move a muscle, often times not even able to talk and you know exactly what's going on. There's something to be said for the oblivion of Alzheimer's – at least they aren't continuously aware of what's going on.

So yeah, I had a pretty good idea of what that meant. But, my initial reaction was to resist, resist, resist. It's what I do best. No way is somebody going to tell me that my beloved husband was going down this road.

So just FYI, you get a diagnosis of cancer, not necessarily so bad. You get a diagnosis of ALS; it's as bad as it gets and here I thought I was the heroine of this story-- not even a little. Dear God, did I even have one iota of the strength that this would take? I really didn't know if I could live up to the vows I had taken. For better or worse, and in sickness and in health. Sounded good at the altar, but I'd read the Joy Fielding book, and I was scared beyond all reason.

I hadn't had children for a reason. I had no desire or interest in being responsible for another human being. At the time, I had absolutely no idea how responsible I'd become and that's probably the only reason we're still married, because running for the hills would have been a pretty reasonable response now that I know what I know.

Chapter Thirteen

I will never forget that morning as long as I live. David went to see the neurologist much like dead man walking. I could have climbed up Mount Everest without oxygen between the hyperkinetic energy and the gasping sound I was making with each breath, sucking in all the life I could, thinking about the possibilities this appointment had in store for both of us.

When he walked in the door I actually hit the floor. I just knew by his face that his worst fears had been preliminarily confirmed.

"What did he say?" I croaked, praying and begging God in my mind for a different answer than the one David had given me the night before.

"It's ALS. Get up," he said.

"No, no, no," I sobbed.

Just for the record, I don't sob as a rule.

"Get up, you're not helping," he said in that weirdly calm voice.

I did get up, but I couldn't even touch him I was so paralyzed (really, no pun intended) by the fear. What happens next? How do you even process news this bad? How do you even get out of the kitchen and move again. What was I supposed to do to comfort him? Did he even want comfort? Who handles this for you? Was I supposed to be in charge? Could I ask myself anymore questions at the same time and not have an answer for one of them?

This all happened in a matter of about five minutes, yet it felt like in those moments I was having a flash forward of how I was now watching a long, slow train wreck. I had to get a grip. I was definitely not helping. David went to check his email. Could you blame him? Normal had definitely left the building.

So I did what I do. I tried to call Dad. He'd know what to do. I for sure didn't. Nobody, and I mean nobody I knew had gotten news this scary, horrible ever. I mean, of course, people had gotten news like this, just not anybody in my lucky life.

I got Mom on the phone and God knows she maintained some semblance of okayness. I think I could have called her and told her I was having a litter of puppies and she might have been less shocked than she probably was, but it's that shock that takes you through those first few phone calls. Now I was the weirdly calm one.

"Your Dad's in Washington, but I'll get in touch with him and we'll call you back," she said.

My guess is that she might have pretty much been close to hitting the floor too. But she called him in D.C. and got him out of some meeting to share this unbelievable news.

Now you have to understand that at this point Dad is the President of the American College of Obstetricians and Gynecologists. It's the mac daddy of positions within his profession. He's the king of the hill. It's something he earned and strived for and damn sure deserved and God knows you talk about raining on someone's parade.

Mom got him on the phone and he told her, "I'm getting on a plane as soon as I can and I'm going straight to Greenville."

"No, they've got to have some time by themselves to deal with this," she told him.

She had predicted that this would be Dad's reaction and I knew I had to head him off so that David could just sit with this for at least a matter of hours.

At some point that afternoon, my friend Carol called. I had completely forgotten that we had talked about meeting them in Charleston that weekend. I'm not sure how I could have possibly forgotten that. When I told her what was going on she literally hung up on me. I understood. Oh, to be able to hang up the phone and walk away from this news.

So the afternoon passed and at some point David had left. I knew where he was. He was driving. That's what he did when he was upset. He drove. The immediate thought that crossed my mind was what would he do when he couldn't drive anymore? Dear God, how fast and furious does the worst case scenario come screaming at you?

I've now had to deal with a diagnosis of cancer and the diagnosis of ALS. Give me cancer any damn day. It honestly never crossed my mind when it was me that I was going to die of cancer. I can honestly say that it crossed my mind that with a diagnosis of ALS I might die -- of a broken heart. And that day my heart started its slow shatter.

Chapter Fourteen

That has to be the longest day in my life and I can only guess that David's day was longer. He never did, and never will, delve into those "feelings" and I couldn't press him. Not now. My desire to talk this thing to death and figure it out really needed to take a backseat to what he needed. And at that point, what he needed was for me to shut up.

Dad called us back and, much like in my situation, needed further confirmation that the diagnosis of ALS was really in fact true.

"Do you want me to get him an appointment up here (at Duke) for a second opinion?" he asked us.

"Hell yeah," was David's first emotional response of any kind.

"Let me make some calls and I'll call you back," Dad said.

It bears mentioning that much like the suck timing of my diagnosis right before Christmas ten months before, David was diagnosed the day before his 43rd birthday. Wow, now there's a gift that just keeps on giving. I was starting to believe that we'd both done something pretty damn bad in a previous life for it all to fall apart at the warp speed things were occurring.

So Dad got him an appointment for mid-October. Now if I thought waiting for appointments and results was excruciating for me in my situation, waiting for answers and information for David was ten million times worse.

Remember, my only benchmark for ALS was a novel I had read years before, but for some reason that book had remained stuck in my head all that time unlike anything I can ever remember reading before or after. I could remember the desperation of the main character, the frustration, the sadness, the hopelessness. I wasn't the one with the diagnosis, but I was sure feeling all those things and more.

My parents came to Greenville that next weekend. Now that was one big, fat barrel of laughs. Nobody could get it together. I can vividly remember sitting on the patio with my parents. David was pretty out of it and more or less just isolating himself despite any of our efforts.

I can remember as if it were yesterday, the utter panic my Mom was trying so desperately to hide and the utter defeat that my Dad was trying so desperately to disguise. Her manic body language, coupled with his elbows on his knees and bent head said more than they ever meant to. Geez, this so doesn't come with a manual. When you get a diagnosis like ALS all you hear is DEATH, DEATH, DEATH. There ain't no dodging this bullet.

"There's a lot of suicide associated with a disease like this," Dad said with such hurt and anguish.

"I know," I said, remembering that was the outcome in what I'll now just refer to as The Book.

It's important for you to know that my parents and David had a preternaturally close relationship for in-laws. David's mother had died several years before, and he and his Dad, well suffice it to say there wasn't a lot of love lost there.

He and Dad spent a lot of time together up at their mountain house, fishing, playing golf, working on the boat. Just stuff guys do. Neither one of them could be accused of being exceedingly conversational most of the time. Mom and I used to laugh at the fact that we were sure they were going to bore each other to death. What they had was the sort of comfortable relationship where conversation just wasn't necessary.

And then there was David and Mom. At one point several years before all of this, Mom had gone to some presentation on one of their travels and the subject was all about categorizing your identity. Whatever. Why she sat through this was beyond me at the time.

So I was sort of laughing at her while she was telling me this on the phone and I yelled out to David.

"Mom doesn't know what her identity is," I said.

There was a short pause and David said, "Tell her she's a goddess mother-in-law."

Okay, they were bonded for life, whether or not that was his intention. He always made a point at Christmas and at other times to buy her gifts that he picked out himself and were just for her from him. Did I mention that his status in the will passed me and probably everyone else?

The bottom line is that we were all in such pain. No way to help David, no way to help ourselves. Just raw, heart-stopping, endless pain.

Finally, David's appointment at Duke was the next day. We drove to Durham to spend the night. It's hard to remember the details of that time, because I was just trying to hold myself together for David's sake. The last thing he needed was me falling apart. And I started what was to become a very, very bad habit – the attitude that "there is no crying with ALS."

The next day David and my Dad set off together for his appointment. Again, he didn't want me to go. He was scheduled to have a test called an electromyogram, or EMG. This test measures the signals that run between nerves and muscles and the electrical activity inside muscles to see if there's a pattern consistent with ALS.

That's the clinical description. The actual description is that they stick needles in your muscles in order to monitor the conductivity of the nerves. From the little I got from David it was hellish and it lasted somewhere in the neighborhood of two hours. Think dentist hitting a nerve over and over and over. With no anesthesia.

They were gone for what seemed like forever. Mom and I were clinging to the very, very faint hope that they would come home with some magical news that it was something else. Something curable, something manageable. I was ragged.

They finally got back and there was not a single doubt that it wasn't good news. Dad was by himself.

"It's ALS," said Dad with such a heave of his breath that I thought we all just might die that very moment.

I was so tense that I thought that I could crack up into a million pieces and never be able to put myself back together again. Mom just looked like her world had ended.

"Where's David? " I managed to get out.

"He's driving," Dad said.

Chapter Fifteen

As seemingly unconcerned and glib as I was about my own little journey with cancer, David's situation was proving to be a whole different beast. And the thing is that I was glib and unconcerned. To this day, everybody seems to think that I buried all kinds of deep seated feelings about my bout with cancer. They want me to acknowledge and explore the pain and the loss. I'm sorry, I'm just not there. Never was.

Call it naiveté, call it ignorance, but it just really didn't occur to me that I was facing anything life threatening. I had no intention whatsoever of dying of that stinking disease. It just seemed wholly inconvenient to me. David's situation sort of went beyond inconvenient. It was inconceivable.

So we went home and everything seemed so different. Like we had walked back into some strangers' home. The kitchen didn't seem welcoming. Our safe stool-sitting counter just seemed sterile. The whole house seemed alien. Already I was picturing in my head the unworkableness of this house. Steep driveway. Steps everywhere. Old house, narrow hallways and doorways. How the hell would you put a ramp anywhere to accommodate a wheelchair to get in and out? As I said, how fast do the worst case scenarios come screaming at you? For the life of me I couldn't get my feet back under me. I'd never felt so helpless in my life.

The doctor David saw at Duke recommended that we look into being seen at the ALS clinic in Charlotte. It was supposed to be one of the best in the country and at the time there were less than 50 dedicated ALS centers in the country. Well isn't that just convenient as all get out. We'd met in Charlotte and it was only about an hour and a half away from Greenville. Dad was on the case. He was going to call the doctor who headed up the center and see if we could be seen. Even Dad couldn't pull those strings.

The way the center works is that they have a clinic once a month and patients rotate through on a quarterly basis. The first opening they had for a new patient was the first week in December. The clinic is what I'll call one stop shopping. You show up and patients (like 40 of them each clinic) see all the doctors and therapists under one roof, in one day. Neurology, gastroenterology, respiratory, speech, occupation and physical therapists. Nutritionists and social workers.

The whole concept makes a tremendous amount of sense when you get right down to it. Instead of having endless appointments, concerns can be addressed on the spot with all of the professionals working together on the patient's plan. Hey, that would mean the left hand knew what the right hand was doing. There's an idea.

But, it just didn't suit me. I was once again in go mode. I wanted immediate gratification and I mean immediate. I wanted action – a feeling that we were actually doing something. Dad had talked with the nurse coordinator as well as the woman who headed up clinical trials. With a disease like ALS, Dad didn't feel there was any immediate danger of waiting a month or so to get in the rotation.

But I wanted to get something, anything going. So I called the nurse to ask some questions of my own. Already David's voice was really becoming affected and talking on the phone was one of the difficulties that had quickly manifested.

When I talked with Ann, the nurse, about David she referred me to Amy, the speech therapist. I should tell you in advance that at that time pretty much everybody that worked for the clinic were named Amy. There was Amy, the speech therapist; Amy, the nutritionist; Amy, the social worker. It was pretty easy for us to remember names.

Anyway I talked with Amy about whether it would make sense for David to try and hook up with a local speech therapist so he could get a head start. Her answer was the first wall we hit.

"There's really no speech therapy that reverses what's happening," she explained.

It wasn't her intention to cut us off, because I will give these people all the credit in the world for putting forth every option, idea and never dampening your hope. They were and are the most caring, dedicated group of therapists, nurses and physicians I've ever encountered -- that first and foremost put the patient first – always first. There were times during all this I wished that maybe for a second I could be first. But I wasn't their responsibility, David was.

"But," she went on, "there are tons of options to help with communication. Technology has come so far and I'll be meeting with you when you come in December and we can figure out if we've got something that might help."

She transferred me to Amber, not another Amy, but another A name. Why this was so funny to me I don't know. It just seemed weird.

Amber is the occupational therapist. I asked her if there was anything specific that David should or could be doing.

"How's his grip?" she asked.

I turned to David to ask him and for the first time realized that the only time I got information from him about what was going on was when somebody medical asked a specific question. I hadn't noticed any real symptoms aside from his voice up to this point.

"It's a little weak," he answered.

I passed that on to Amber and she suggested that using one of those little squeezy balls was good exercise. Okay, now that's more like it. I was starting to get a sip, not a taste yet, but a nibble of what being an advocate/caregiver for someone chronically ill was going to be like. I already thought that I probably wasn't going to be so hot at this.

Chapter Sixteen

Before I knew it Thanksgiving was right around the corner. My parents had planned a family vacation for all of us, including my brother Chuck, his wife Ann, and my niece and nephews, Katie, 9, Charlie,10 and Oliver, 6, to Jamaica. Since it was planned before we knew what was going on with David, I suppose it was originally going to be sort of a celebration of the end of my treatment. Instead, it had taken a decidedly different turn.

Now you have to remember that at this point my hair was just starting to grow back in. It was some kind of weird ashy color and was so curly. I barely recognized myself. But the fact is that while I could have worn my wig and looked like my old self, after all the stuff we'd been going through with David, my hair seemed fairly insignificant. Screw it. I would just look horrible – at least in my own opinion and -- apparently the customs agent agreed.

So we're going through customs in the Jamaica airport and the guy takes my passport, which of course had a picture of my former blonde, straight-haired self on it. I may not have mentioned it but I also lost a pretty decent amount of weight during treatment, which was really a good thing. I wasn't gaunt, just thinner.

"This isn't you," he said in that lilting accent.

"Uh, yeah it is," I said.

"No, this definitely isn't you," he replied in a less charming lilt.

I was not feeling all kinds of welcomed to Jamaica.

"I had cancer and my hair is just growing back," I said as I fought back tears.

This was bordering on humiliating.

"Oh, okay, welcome to Jamaica," he said, sliding my passport back to me.

Up yours.

We were staying at the Ritz-Carlton and it was exquisitely beautiful. And it was all inclusive, which might have been a miscalculation on their part because I'm pretty sure we drank our weight and more every day. I think they were pulling up with tanker trucks of Red Stripe beer daily.

It was almost like everybody just needed to be somewhere completely different that even for a brief moment provided an escape from our "new" normal. The kids were really too young to grasp what was going on with David, but they, as kids often do, had an almost eerie sensitivity to the fact that this trip was special.

There were so many instances I can remember. Like the first night we were there. Chuck and crew had gotten in later than us so we just met them at dinner. Hugs all around and that comforting feeling that we were all together.

"Hey, Katie, how awful is this hair?" I said pointing to my head.

"Not awful. Different, but cute," she answered without missing a beat.

That same night after dinner the kids were dying, dying, dying to go down and see the beach. So we all walked down and took our shoes off and dipped our feet in the warm surf. The kids were insanely happy, so much so that the next thing we knew they were in the water, fully clothed, splashing, screaming and celebrating the simplest of life's pleasures. And as if to add icing to the cake, my brother jumped in with them. Perfect.

I'm not much of a beach sitter, but David was in a big way. And every day, the kids would run out to the beach and knowing David would be there later, would make sure they got him a chair. So he hung with them and while I can't say for sure, he seemed to get some much needed energy from their liveliness and abundant joy.

There were intentionally funny moments and unintentionally funny moments. David always looked like he was burned to a crisp after a day in the sun, but by the next day he was just tanned and healthy looking. I always just stayed burned looking.

Anyway, the first evening after a full day on the beach we were all gathered in my parents' room before we went to dinner and my mother said, "Oooh David. You are so burned. You've got to use sunscreen. I don't want you getting skin cancer."

David just looked at her with a deadpan face and said, "Yeah, that would be just awful."

We all died laughing despite the black humor. Poor Mom, she looked like she had just stepped in something. But, the good thing was that we were all laughing and somehow we knew we weren't going to have to walk on eggshells all the time. That even though the situation was dire, we weren't going to chuck our senses of humor and go to the dark side. Thank God for that.

December came roaring up on us after our trip and we were off to Charlotte for David's first visit to the ALS Clinic. I think we were both frightened and hopeful at the same time. David had spent a lot of time online looking for various drug trials and anything that might be out there. Something I had stayed far, far away from. But he seemed to have some kind of attitude adjustment and was at least looking forward in a more proactive way than before.

I gotta tell you, walking into that waiting room with 30 or 40 patients in various stages of ALS could take your breath away. It was like watching a movie that was playing, "this is your life, get used to it and it's gonna suck." It was terrifying and I do not know to this day how David didn't run screaming into the traffic outside.

So we started seeing the various doctors and therapists and they were piling information and tools and tricks on us at warp speed.

Social worker Amy got us up to speed on the ins and outs of Social Security Disability. Not a small task. She explained that with ALS you can extend your health insurance through Cobra an additional 11 months, which is sort of great and sick all at the same time. The insurance company sort of gives you a break because they're pretty much betting you won't be around long enough to take advantage of it. She was just an incredible wealth of information that was so infinitely helpful there are really no words to describe it.

Nutritionist Amy was concerned about David's weight loss over the past couple of months. She was one of those "we" talkers which drove us both insane and made us completely avoid eye contact with each other for fear of laughing out loud.

"What are 'we' eating these days? Would we be interested in a food supplement that adds calories? We really need to add and maintain weight because it's really hard to reverse," she droned.

As we left her, David looked at me and asked, "Do you think we could go screw ourselves?"

And on it went. It really blew by quickly and David even signed up to participate in a clinical trial of a new experimental drug. This really was a case of what's to lose?

While nothing was really different than when we went in, we came out of that visit a little less scared, a little less off-balance. While there may be no cure for ALS, these people we'd just spent a day with cared so much about the patients' quality of life that we knew that at least we had a place to turn with our questions, challenges and needs. There's something to be said for not feeling like we were so alone in dealing with all this.

Chapter Seventeen

Well about now you're probably thinking, "this story is so *not* sounding lucky." But, as I found out over and over again, just when I'd start feeling overwhelmed and completely out of my depth, something or someone came along to jolt me back to my lucky feeling self.

As I mentioned, I went to college in Charlotte and still had a number of friends from back in the day. Specifically there was Cam. She and I been roommates in school, and for years on and off after graduation. We laugh and say we're the sisters we never wanted.

You know how difficult that roommate stuff can be. It just never was with Cam and me. It was remarkably easy even though we were so different in a lot of ways. There was the physical. I was 5'7". She was 5'1" on a tall day. She was tender-hearted. I was sarcastic. (Well okay she can hold her own in the sarcasm department, but she'd cry at things way, way faster than I would. I mean *Little House on the Prairie* could bring her to her knees.) We just got each other.

While we'd stayed in touch through the years there were times we were closer than others. No animosity or discord, just timing and circumstance. But we were always, always able to pick up right where we left off with no recriminations, blame or finger pointing.

Apparently, we'd sort of been out of touch longer than usual. I hadn't been able to go to her wedding a few years before due to a wicked case of strep throat and geez, I hadn't even met her husband. I thought about her a lot and missed her a lot, but we just seemed to be figuratively and literally in different places and life just kept getting in the way.

She happened to call me out of the blue not too long after David's diagnosis and for whatever reason I hadn't called her when I was going through my cancer treatment so we maybe had a little catching up to do. There wasn't any reason that I didn't call her other than I was just so massively hammered with everything going on that I couldn't go through it with another soul.

Well, didn't she just have her own bombshell to drop.

"Hey bud. I've got some news," said her oh, so familiar voice.

Yeah, me too I thought to myself. Hope yours is better than mine.

"I've got a baby," she said laughing.

Huuuuuuuh????? If I'd said it out loud, I would have sounded like Scooby Doo at his most surprised.

Cam hadn't gotten married until she was almost forty so at this point she was around forty-three.

"What? When," I said in utter disbelief.

"She was born in May and her name is Samantha, after my dad," she said.

She went on to tell me all about her wonderful news and the joy and excitement was such a tonic to my pain that I knew at that moment that I would never let her get too far away from me ever again. Ever.

Then it was my turn.

———————

Talk about raining on somebody's parade. Catching Cam up on the events of the past year was so awful and such a relief at the same time. I had my Cam back. And she had a baby. And I had a dying husband. We're only one month apart age-wise. My God, how did we both get here?

Her innate understanding of me seemed to take over. I didn't have to explain everything to death. The comfort I felt from our conversation gave me new energy that I could do this. She's always given me credit for stuff I never give myself credit for. She's been a cheerleader, but at the same time she's honest to a fault. Almost blunt sometimes, but isn't that what makes cherished friends the ones you want around when things are the roughest?

The company Cam was working for was ironically headquartered in Greenville, though they lived in Charlotte, and Cam wanted immediately to plan a visit to see us both.

"Would David mind? I just need to see him," she asked.

One thing I can tell you about Cam is that there's nothing that is too tough for her. She goes head-first into even the most difficult situations and facing David in this situation was not easy, as evidenced by many people who, over the course of his illness, fell away.

Not Cam. Within a couple of weeks she came through town and came by the house and had a visit with David and was so sweet and compassionate that once again, I knew I needed more than just an occasional phone call with her and I think that's when the seed of moving back to Charlotte was subconsciously planted.

So we picked up where we left off and at just the right time. I had always thought of myself as pretty self-sufficient, but now more than ever it was dawning on me that I couldn't do this alone, or even just with David. Or even with me, David and my family. Friends were going to be critical to my survival.

———

So a few months later when we headed back to Charlotte, I called Cam and asked if she and Jamie, her husband I'd never met, wanted to meet us for a drink at out hotel.

"Sure, we've got to bring Samantha. Is that okay" she asked.

Of course it was okay. My friend had a husband and a baby I'd never met. David, never all that kid-oriented, was cool with it too. And he wasn't at his most social as you might imagine.

I'll never forget meeting Jamie that first time. It was as if I had known him as long as I'd known Cam. And David, even as crazed as he was with worry and weariness, immediately warmed to both Jamie and Samantha. He always had a special place for Cam.

There are moments frozen in time that always stay with you. I'll never forget that night, as simple and uncomplicated as it could be, even with a toddler crawling around us. It was relaxing. We hadn't done anything this normal in weeks, if not months. Even David seemed to relish the normalcy of just having drinks with friends.

Samantha climbed in my lap and I gave her my bracelet to play with. She was angelic that night as we had that "getting to know you" conversation, which should have happened long before, but was made more poignant due to the urgency of time. Time that was cloudy. Time that was unknown. Time that was fleeting.

That night we didn't just reconnect with a friend and her family. It was so much more than that because unbeknownst to us, we had started down the path to becoming a part of that family. Lucky us.

Chapter Eighteen

Over the next couple of months we struggled to figure out how to deal with our new normal. David's company had put him on short-term disability in December when it became painfully obvious that a sales rep who couldn't talk was not a great plan. Along with his speech problems, the fatigue that he was experiencing was also incredibly debilitating. So he wasn't working and that was just another loss to adapt to.

I know during that time I felt like I was under water. It was like I was seeing everything through this blurry curtain. I was afraid <u>all</u> the time. Yet I felt like I had to swim through it for David's sake. My emotions were on a hair trigger. For God's sake there was a Prego spaghetti sauce commercial that for some reason had the saddest music and every time it came on I burst into tears. That didn't seem all that normal to me and I knew I was going to have to get it together one way or another.

By March it was time to go back up to Charlotte for another visit to the ALS clinic. I was still at a point that those appointments gave me some hope for solutions to the challenges that seemed to be flying at us every other day.

There was the issue of David falling. Which he did -- a lot. I don't know how parents of toddlers don't lose their minds when their kids start to walk. I guess kids don't have as far to fall and they shake it off a little better. Honestly every time David walked through the house or out to the car in our ridiculously steep driveway or even up the back steps to take the garbage to our can, I held my breath.

On a funny note though, Betty and Peggy, our dogs, had learned to give him a wide berth – if he was going down it wasn't going to be on them. Then there was the time that David stood up and Peggy launched herself off the couch at him like a fifteen pound bowling ball and literally knocked him over flat on his back. I was in my office behind the living room and heard what happened, but didn't see it. Betty obviously saw it because she hightailed herself into the office and got under my desk. She wasn't having any part of that action.

If this all sounds kind of crazy, it was, but I was hopeful that we might get some answers to help us deal with this. David had started using a cane, which maybe it's just me but I just really don't get the point of a cane. He still fell, now he just had something to try not to fall on. It just didn't seem all that helpful. Maybe the ALS people would have some better suggestions.

They did. They thought using one of those rolly walkers would be a good idea to help make him safer. I didn't say a word. Every time David had to make another adjustment or adapt to his new limitations, he didn't exactly embrace it. Already that day he had nixed the idea of using a speech device.

"Why?" you're probably asking.

I have some theories on that because David's reasoning was never very clear to me. He would tell whatever therapist who had some suggestion that he'd think about it and then it would just sort of be off the table for discussion. I think every time he had to face either some new technology or adapt to a new way to handle basic every day activities he felt one step closer to death. So why not put it off? I, on the other hand, was starting to feel so frustrated.

"How can you not take advantage of this?" I asked impatiently after one appointment.

"It would totally help you," I pressed

"Not your decision," he answered.

"Damn right it isn't my decision, but this crap that affects you, affects me too," I fired back.

This was the beginning of what was to ultimately become a pattern. I would be the glass half full optimistic one (bully for me) and he would resist, resist, resist (who could blame him).

Anyway, when she suggested the rolling walker I just knew he was going to blow her off. And then lo and behold, he capitulated and said he'd give it a try. Thank you God, thank you God, thank you God. I truly couldn't believe that he was on board with this. But I guess if you fall and bust your ass enough times you might be more open to trying something else.

Now there was one little problem with this new development. Most people have a pretty good idea how crazy Jack Russell terriers are. Hand grenades with teeth is a pretty good description. And they are especially crazy when it comes to anything with wheels.

The vacuum cleaner, the lawn mower, you name it and they go nuts barking, biting trying to stop it. So this could be problematic. Just what David needed was two fifteen pound speed bumps running interference. Yikes.

"D, what do you think the dogs are going to do when they see this?" I asked as we drove back to Greenville.

"Probably go insane," he laughed.

"I'll take it in and give them a treat and maybe it won't be so bad and they'll get used to it quicker," he said.

So we took the walker in and unfolded it in the kitchen and just waited to see what their reaction would be. Not much interest initially, so David gave them a treat. Then he stood behind it and began to walk toward them, wheels rolling. Nothing. Unbelievably there was zero barking, biting or commotion of any kind. It was as if they instinctively knew that David needed the walker and they weren't going to cause any problem. Wow.

———

Another conversation we had on the way back from that trip to Charlotte was going to have a much bigger impact on us.

"Would you ever consider moving back to Charlotte?" David asked me.

"Uh, yeah in a skinny minute," I answered.

I wasn't kidding. Our house was becoming increasingly more difficult to live in. There were stairs and more stairs. Our driveway was like a Swiss Alp, only made of asphalt. David had already fallen out there and broken his collar bone. We probably looked like two drunks that day with me trying to help him up and trying not to fall backwards myself. Ramping that house to accommodate the inevitable wheelchair was virtually impossible to picture. There really was not one thing that was keeping us in Greenville.

"What about you?" I asked.

"Yeah, I love it there," he replied.

Oh yeah, talk about planting a seed, hell he'd planted a fifteen foot sapling. The idea spun around in my head. We'd be closer to my parents. We'd be closer to good friends. We'd be close to the ALS Center. I would get out of Godforsaken Greenville. Yahoo!

Now it was a matter of logistics. How to make it happen? If I can say one thing about myself it's that if I want something, no matter how big, I can absolutely make it happen. So I was off and running, at least in my head. This was good. This was hope. This was fun. Fun? Oh yeah, something positive to focus on. Something that would be good for both of us. Fun. Hadn't had much of that lately. I felt something in me lighten. The awful suffocating feeling wasn't quite so heavy. The blurry curtain was maybe just a teensy bit clearer. Yep, this was exactly what we needed.

Chapter Nineteen

Under most circumstances the thought of moving would seem like a big, fat chore. Not in our case. I knew with 100 percent certainty that we were supposed to do this. But, I also knew that we were going to need a lot of help and that there would be any number of tricky obstacles that could trip us up. David was really not going to be able to physically help me with getting the house ready to sell. Nor would he have the stamina to make endless trips to Charlotte to look at houses. And then there was that pesky idea of getting a mortgage.

Banks are funny about lending money. This was before all the crazy sub-prime insanity, so they were kind of picky about oh, I don't know, things like having jobs. We had income thanks to disability insurance and Social Security, but to a lender we weren't exactly looking like the picture of stability.

The good news was that our house was in a fantastic location and we were poised to make a fairly decent profit in the ten or so years we'd been there. The other good news was that my parents are remarkable people who just jumped in and told us they would do whatever it took to help us. And they did. There really are no words to describe the unconditional support they provided us. Suffice it to say that this move would <u>not</u> have happened without them. So with their encouragement we were able to start the ball rolling.

The first thing I did was start cleaning closets and de-junking. Ugh. Now that was a chore. How do you accumulate so much crap? David even tried to start cleaning the closet in his office. It was heartbreaking to watch. In addition to the speech difficulties he was literally losing his grip. Even picking up file folders was a struggle. But, I could tell he just wanted to <u>do</u> something, anything. So I just stayed out of his way until I just couldn't stand it.

"Hon, I love you for trying to do this, but you're exhausting yourself," I said as gently as I could.

His frustration was as evident as his despair. I knew what he was thinking.

"For God's sake I can't even throw file folders in the trash. What good am I?"

I hugged him close and didn't say a word.

Slowly but surely I got things organized. I had bags of crap everywhere, upstairs, downstairs, in the basement, and not a single idea of what to do with it when I saw this truck beside me one day when I was running errands. The sign on it said 1-800-Got-Junk. I went home and called them. All I had to do was schedule a pick-up time and they would come and load everything, and I mean everything into their truck. It didn't have to be packaged any certain way or even at all. Of course there was a fee for this, but it wasn't exorbitant and just the manpower alone was worth the price. This may be the single best company in the world. I love, love, love these people.

They came and within an incredibly short period of time my piles disappeared. Lord love 'em. They even swept my garage. Huh? Are you kidding me? On the off chance you didn't get this, I would highly recommend 1-800-Got-Junk.

So with that accomplished, I called our neighbor who had actually sold us the house initially. She came over and met with us to get it listed. She was floored when she realized what was going on with us. Our neighborhood was friendly, we just weren't very involved with each other.

We got the contract done and as we stood to walk her out, David fell. Just lost his balance getting up and hit the floor. He couldn't get up. I will give this lady credit. She looked at me and said, "You get under one arm and I'll get the other." And damn if we didn't hoist him back up to the chair. If she didn't know it before she knew it now – she was going to <u>earn</u> her money on this sale.

Anybody who has ever sold a house knows what a gigantic pain in the butt it is. Keeping it clean for showings. Having to get out when there were showings. And in our case that was no small feat. Every time we had a showing I had to help David get down the stairs and into the car without falling. It scared me beyond belief and the process took fifteen or twenty minutes. Then I had to load the dogs in the car because they couldn't be there either. And then we would have to just drive around for however long it took because we couldn't just leave the dogs in a hot car. Pure fun. It was horrible. David felt bad, I felt guilty for feeling frustrated and the dogs, well they just thought they were going to the vet every time so they were insane in the car.

During this same time my friend Carol in Atlanta had hooked me up with a real estate agent in Charlotte. Nancy was actually retired, but she referred me to a close friend who worked for the same company. Her name was Judy Perrell and once again luck was with me. She was (and is) fabulous. Funny, smart and totally on top of things. She also has a daughter with Multiple Sclerosis so she completely understood the strict parameters we had about which houses would work. Master on the main floor, large enough halls and doorways to accommodate a wheelchair and the ability to build a ramp. Not necessarily the easiest assignment. I talked with her and arranged for us to meet after David's next clinic so we could start looking at houses.

I also asked my Mom to come so that I would have another opinion. David would ride with us, but the task of getting in and out of the car and in and out of houses was just going to be too much for him. It was weird to think about picking out a house kind of by myself. David and I had always been such a team.

So after David finished his appointment, we met Mom and Judy at the hotel and off we went. Poor Mom, she loves looking at houses and going through every room and really digesting it all. I, on the other hand, can decide within approximately 30 seconds if I'm interested. Some of them I didn't even want to get out of the car. So we stopped at one house and I knew instantly I hated it, and Judy, being the highly intuitive person she is had already figured out how to read me.

"Oh let's just take a quick look inside," said Mom.

Since she'd gone to the trouble to come and help it seemed like the least I could do. So in we went. I walked in the door and just rolled my eyes, while Mom had already gone to see the rest.

"Run, Peggy run, Sharon's out of here," shouted Judy, laughing.

I think Mom decided then and there that I was absolutely zero fun to look at houses with and who could blame her. While she would have come with me again, I knew I would drive her crazy, and I was moving fast, in and out of town fairly often and she couldn't just drop everything at a moment's notice to get to Charlotte. We decided to let me look and if we narrowed it down to something doable, then Mom and/or Dad could come.

I feel like I looked at a thousand houses. There was the one that looked okay enough from the outside, but we got inside and each and every room was painted a different neon color. I know, it's only paint, but with all we had on our plate, redoing a house just wasn't in the cards. There was the older home that would have had to have a complete bathroom overhaul. And then finally there was the completely handicapped accessible perfect, perfect home.

It had a ramp from the garage into the house. It had a gigantic master bedroom on the main floor with a gigantic bathroom that you could actually roll a shower chair in and out of. It had plenty of room to maneuver around. It was made to order.

It was exactly what we were looking for, with the exception of a fence for our dogs. The house was in a subdivision that would obviously have a homeowners' association so Judy suggested driving around to see if there were other fences in the neighborhood. There were. So she got in touch with the President of the HOA to ask about it. He gave her a flat no. He said they'd revised their covenants and wouldn't allow fences anymore.

Judy pled our cause to him, explained our situation, told him we would let them approve any design and the rat bastard still said no. I hold a grudge against him to this day. But like they say, if it wasn't meant to be it wasn't meant to be. I didn't feel very consoled.

Chapter Twenty

The search continued for the right house and I can tell you I was getting crazed. Our house in Greenville wasn't exactly flying off the market. We had one offer pretty much right off the bat, from a youth minister and his wife. We got all the way to setting a closing date when they balked.

Peggy, our real estate agent called me.

"Um, Sharon, they've decided to back out of the deal. He said he prayed about it and decided they shouldn't buy the house," she said

"Fine, give me his earnest money check and tell him to pray I don't find him," I seethed.

"Well, there's a problem with that. His wife never signed the contract and I didn't have any reason to think there was going to be a problem so unfortunately I never followed up. It was never valid," she tried to explain.

I could feel my head exploding. She was on her way out. I was pissed, frustrated and just sick of the whole thing. I had to remind myself that I was doing the work on the front end for the pay-off on the back end. Get through this crap and get ourselves to Charlotte. If only we could find a stinking house.

Several more weeks went by and there were no other serious offers. I decided that since her listing contract was almost up we were just going to have to take the house off the market until we could get out of there. We had already had to cancel one appointment when David fell again and I couldn't get him up in time. Aargh. It was all too much.

By this point our house was just becoming a monster to manage. David was sleeping downstairs in our guest room, because the steps were just too tricky. It just didn't seem fair on any level (no pun intended). I would have moved down there with him, but the room could only hold a full size bed and we would have been even more miserable trying to cram in there. It was awful. So everyone was working as hard as possible to find us a house.

While David couldn't make these spur of the minute trips, what he could do was scour the internet for possibilities. And he did. He spent hours online. Dad, meanwhile would get the Charlotte newspaper every weekend and go through the real estate section to see what he could find. (If you can believe it not one place in Greenville carried the *Charlotte Observer*.) Judy, meanwhile was looking as hard as anybody possibly could. I don't know how she had time for other clients with all the time she spent on us.

I swear on everything I hold dear that this next part really, actually happened.

"Sharon, come here," David yelled from my office. "I think I may have found something."

I walked in and he pointed to the picture of an adorable house on the screen.

"It says it's in Cotswold," he said.

Cotswold was one of our top choices of locations in Charlotte. Close in, very convenient but with many houses out of our price range or rehabs that were just too much to take on.

"Yeah, right. There's gotta be a catch," I said, not daring to get my hopes up.

The phone rang and it was Judy.

"Sharon, I think I found something," she said excitedly.

"Cool, so did David. Can you check them both out," I answered.

"Yeah, what's the address of the one David found?" she asked.

"626," I began

"Queen Charlotte's Ct.," she finished.

Astonishingly, they had both happened upon the same exact house. Judy said she was going right then to check it out for us to see if it was worth a trip. Less than an hour later she called me and I knew from her voice that we may have finally hit the jackpot.

"When can you get here," she said without preamble.

"I can be there first thing tomorrow," I answered, praying I wouldn't be disappointed.

"Perfect, I'll see you then," she said.

So I met her in Charlotte and we went to see the house. Ding, ding, ding we have a winner. It wasn't a trick. It would work. Not just work, it was even better than I expected. It was in a fantastic neighborhood cul-de-sac and the whole neighborhood was just beautiful. And as if to put icing on the cake, while Judy was there she met the listing agent by coincidence and he told her they had just reduced the price. She'd also already covered the fence issue and all we had to do was submit our fence plan for approval so that hurdle was cleared. Sweet. For the first time in months I could feel my hopes rising again.

I called my Dad who was on call for me to get in the car and zoom to Charlotte, God bless him. I think he literally hung up, grabbed his keys and came to Charlotte. Since it would take him a couple of hours to get here I went ahead back to Greenville. Waiting for him to call was excruciating. I needed him to agree, but I also needed a level head to make sure I wasn't overlooking anything huge.

"David, it's perfect," I said as I ran in the house. "Dad's on his way to see it. I think this is it."

Finally the phone rang.

"Hey, it's Dad. This is it. I'm ready to put an offer in if you agree," he said.

Yeah, you read that right, my parents were ponying up a mortgage to get us in this house. Of course we'd give them any profits from the sale of our house, but they were shouldering the majority of the responsibility and taking it on themselves and off our backs. Lucky girl.

"Thank you, thank you," I said.

So we made the offer and the owner, Janice, accepted. No games, no back and forth. Everybody plays, everybody wins. A neighbor told me later that when Janice heard our story she said, "They need this house and they are the ones that are supposed to be here." Maybe some things <u>are</u> meant to be.

Dad had proposed a closing date that was going to put me into high gear. But that was all good, the sooner we were out of G'ville, the better. Of course David was very eager to see it in person and for the first time in a pretty good while seemed to feel like he was contributing. I mean really, he found the house for goodness sakes.

Of course the first person I called was Cam.

"We found a house," I said, feeling crazed with joy.

"Where?" she asked.

"Cotswold," I answered.

"Yahoo, you'll be so close to us," she said, as excited as I was.

"We're coming back up there so David can see it. Want to meet us over there?" I asked.

"Absolutely, just tell me when and where," she said.

So Friday came and David and I headed to Charlotte. I was so, so excited for him to see it and love it like I did. And he did. And Cam did. And Samantha even seemed to like it, though she was much more interested in David's rolly walker and having Cam push her around on it. But hey, she was only a kid.

The only other possible snag was the home inspection. Ever the perfect real estate agent, Judy arranged for the inspection and told me not to worry about coming back for it because she would just handle it. Thank the Good Lord, it went smooth as silk.

We had a house. It still makes me smile to remember those feelings. We had new hopes to replace the ones that seemed so far away and long ago. This would be a new start on this new journey we never planned on taking. But it was okay. We had a house.

Chapter Twenty-One

The next few weeks went by in a blur of getting moving estimates, packing and more organization. I was like an insane General directing a full-on assault on Charlotte. I was definitely in go mode. Looking back I think David was pretty much just trying to stay out of my way. I was bordering on manic I was so possessed with getting us out of this house and into the new one.

The expense of moving was definitely not in our budget, but it didn't matter to me. We'd figure it out. One of my many odd jobs was to sell our second car and that seemed like a pretty good way to get a decent chunk of change.

David had pretty much stopped driving at that point and we most certainly didn't need two cars. The awful thing was that of course the one we had to sell was the one David loved – our Isuzu Trooper, because mine was in the middle of a lease. For whatever reason he loved that SUV so much, but he realized that there wasn't any way to keep it, much less pay to move it. Another loss for him on a list that was getting way, way too long. So I had to figure out how to sell it.

We thought about putting it in the paper and quickly dismissed that idea when weirdly, at the same time, a prominent man from Greenville was kidnapped and killed while meeting someone to sell his Suburban. It was an awful story. He met them in a public place and this couple knocked him over the head, shoved him in their van and then taped his mouth shut. He suffocated and died. Didn't seem like a great idea to put it in the paper.

So I decided to just take it to Carmax and get what I could for it. Since it had been sitting for a while and apparently leaking when it rained, it stunk. A lot. So I got it cleaned up the best I could and set off to sell it.

After what seemed like forever waiting for them to inspect it and get an estimate together two guys came and got me and took me into a private office. The price they offered was so far below what I thought we would get that I promptly burst into tears. Bet they didn't see that coming.

I wasn't just tearing up, I was bawling.

"My husband has Lou Gehrig's disease and we're moving and I thought we'd get more and I just have to call him and see what he thinks," I blubbered at them.

You can imagine their delight at my emotional blackmail. But it wasn't intentional, nor a ploy to get more money, though if that had worked yippee for me. I was just so discouraged and sad and tired. So I called David and the phone rang and rang and rang. No answer. Now I was really crying. What was wrong? Why wasn't he answering?

I hung up and dialed again. Finally he answered. While no one else could understand him on the phone, I could.

"Why didn't you answer?" I said frantically.

"I dropped the phone and it took me a while to get it," he said.

Need I say more?

"They only offered us fifteen hundred bucks for the car," I said. I knew he knew I was crying and that made me feel even worse. Just what he needs. Me crying and him feeling helpless to help me solve these problems.

"Take it. That's probably the best we'll do," he garbled at me.

So I hung up and told the guys that we had a deal. They probably knew that since they'd listened to the whole conversation. Then, even though they couldn't offer me more money, one of the guys said one of the most perceptive and kind things I can remember along the way.

"You're really, really tired of doing things by yourself, aren't you? It's gotta be hard." he said.

Yeah, you could say that.

So the deal was struck, the check was written and my friend picked me up to go home. What a great day. But at least we'd gotten something out of it.

And then out of the blue just a day or so later we got a call from David's former boss.

"Hi Sharon it's Bob," he said when I answered. "I know that David can't really talk on the phone, but could you get him to pick up and just listen?"

"Sure," I replied.

David got on the other phone. I know we were both thinking – where was this going?

"Dave the guys in the sales department got together and we've got a check for you guys for $2,000 dollars. We wanted to do something so you could take a great vacation or whatever," he said, obviously sort of uncomfortable at having been designated the group spokesperson.

"Oh my God. That's the nicest thing I've ever heard," I said.

David managed to get out an understandable "thank you."

Just when you think things are in the toilet, something like this happens. Moving costs covered. Thank you, thank you, thank you.

I lined up the movers and prayed I hadn't signed a contract with a company that was going to hold our stuff hostage. Never had I been so scared. Okay, never in the past two months had I been so scared. Our lives had become one scary day after another.

I have many bad habits, but one that would come back to bite me in the butt was my abhorrence to asking for help. I don't know why or where this came from. I just always felt the need to do it myself or at the minimum with David's help. This move was starting to overwhelm me on so many levels. I ain't big on change and that's all my life was at that point – one 'effing change after another. But, somehow I figured out that I needed reinforcements. My parents were going to be closing on the house at the same time the movers were going to be delivering, so they were otherwise occupied.

So I called my brother. Of course he'd been in the loop for months and was a constant source of support and practical thinking. I'm sure that's why I thought he might be just what we needed to get us through this.

"Hey, it's me. I'm going to ask you a gigantic favor," I said, getting right to it.

"I need you. I can't do this move alone."

"Funny, I was going to call you and volunteer to come help," he said.

Now this isn't like he's just popping over from across town. He lives in Iowa and was a fairly new owner of a business and has a wife and three kids. Just a little busy.

We were scheduled for the mover to pick up our stuff on Thursday and deliver on Friday. Chuck would fly in on Thursday while they were packing up, we'd drive to Charlotte when they were done and he'd fly out of Charlotte on Sunday. God bless him. I could actually feel my stress level drop like a rock. I had back-up coming. Thank God for back-up.

Chapter Twenty-Two

I don't profess to be an expert on caregiving or how to handle a chronic disease, but what I do know for sure is that while on the face of it I appeared to be in control and on top of my game, I was just trying to outrun it all. If I could stay busy enough, create enough chaos and chores for myself, maybe, just maybe, I could keep all the pain and fear at bay. While this move to Charlotte was ultimately going to be a very, very good thing, it was hell right now and to this day I know I could have never pulled it off without Chuck and a lot of other people.

He flew in mid-day on Thursday, the day they were loading all of our stuff onto the truck. Once again, by the grace of God, we had lucked out and got the best movers ever. These guys were so kind and compassionate and funny and they flew like the wind. Without huge explanations, they knew that the chair David was sitting in was going to be the last thing on the truck along with the television. No big deal made, no embarrassment for David.

So I picked Chuck up from the airport and got lunch for everyone and headed back home. Wow, had they made progress. Our plan was when they finished we would head to Charlotte and spend the night at a hotel and meet the guys at our new house the next morning. I like a plan. After just a couple of more hours they had loaded everything and we were ready to go. I couldn't believe it.

I really didn't know how I was going to feel when we left. After all, this was our first house, the one we had loved so much for so long. It was where so much had gone right and so much had gone wrong. I was a tad ambivalent to say the least.

I'll never forget when we got David settled in the car and were backing out of the driveway he said, "Let's drive around and take one more look at the neighborhood."

I was on the verge of a big, ugly cry and just said, "No, let's just get out of here."

It was excruciating to keep from losing it, but I managed and off we went to Charlotte. As usual David seemed to instinctively understand that I was on a very precarious edge and let it go. Chuck got it too and as is his way he made us laugh the whole trip. Without him I think it would have been very different and very dreary.

When I made the hotel reservation I <u>very</u> explicitly requested a handicapped room for David and me, and was repeatedly assured that they would take care of it. We had stayed there before and hadn't had a problem so I wasn't too worried. We got to the hotel, unloaded David's walker and our bags and went to check in. Fine, no problem. We went up the elevator and proceeded to the very furthest room on the hall. And I'm not kidding when I say it was one long, damn hall. And guess what, it wasn't handicapped. So we checked the other room to make sure we hadn't mixed up the keys. Nope, not handicapped.

So we went back downstairs to figure it out. Remember now, we're moving at a snail's pace to accommodate David, plus I was always afraid he was going to fall, and this day had already been exhausting for him. I went to the desk and told the guy our room wasn't handicapped.

"Oh, I didn't realize you needed a handicapped room," he said. "Let me see what else we've got."

I stood there and stood there while he did that ticky type type thing like the airline agents do. I was tired, wanted a drink and really wasn't in the mood. This went on and on. Then he had a sidebar with another check-in gal and finally when I was one second away from going over the counter he handed me a key.

"Okay, here you go," he said.

So up we went again and down the other way to the furthest room on the opposite side of the hotel. At this point Chuck had suggested that David just sit on his rolly walker and was pushing him. And don't forget we're also schlepping our bags and stuff so we looked a little crazy. I opened the door to the new room and I'm pretty sure that my head exploded.

"It's not frigging handicapped," I screamed. "How is David supposed to take a shower or I don't know, use the toilet?"

Chuck just took the key out of my hand and said, "Meet me at the elevator; I'll handle this."

In just a very, very few minutes he was back with yet another key and we were finally set. To this day I don't know what he said to them, but he made it happen quickly and efficiently. This was why I'd called him in the first place. If I'd been by myself, this story probably wouldn't have been written since I was homicidal by then. But it was handled. Oh the relief of just having somebody else crawl through the glass for me.

That night, even with all the crap that had gone on, was just pure fun. We'd stopped and bought beer for Chuck, I had a cooler with wine and grapefruit juice and a flask of vodka for David. We had damn sure earned a few cocktails. We had more than a few. And we laughed. A lot. And we got room service and watched Donald Trump act like a jerk on *The Apprentice*. David was relaxed. I was relaxed. That could have been the cocktails, but then again, I think just having somebody else to shoulder some of this hugeness was like a panacea to both David and me. Maybe a little bit of "misery loves company" but, more like it just didn't seem as gigantic and scary with someone else in the room.

———

The next morning we drove over to the new house. It might be one of the longest days in the history of the world. If I heard one time, I heard it one thousand times.

"Sharon, where does this go? Sharon, where do you want this? Sharon, Sharon, Sharon."

And then finally, the head mover guy looked at me and said, "Hey, Imelda, where do you want these?"

He was holding a gigantic box marked "shoes" and I knew that there was more than one of those and so did he. It was hilarious.

And while it was one of the longest days, the whole weekend was filled with love and hope and laughs.

My friend Chris Stowe showed up ready to work. And work she did for two days straight. She got our bed made up first thing, which by the way if you're ever helping somebody who's moving, is about the kindest thing you can do for them. God, would I need a bed tonight. And not to have to forage for covers was pure magic. She also took charge of keeping my mother focused.

I love my Mom, but she ain't the best multi-tasker. Chris would give her something to do and then watch her get distracted.

"Focus Peg, focus," she kept repeating to her.

Chuck and the cable guy got all our internet and cable TV stuff working, which was also pure magic as that crap makes me insane. Chris's husband, Robert made a trip to Best Buy for stuff Chuck needed and got us all Chinese food for dinner. Judy, our real estate agent sent us a gigantic platter of cold cuts and other goodies for lunch. Family friends, Bob and Sheila actually drove from Spartanburg to Greenville and busted our dogs out of the kennel and drove them up to us in Charlotte to save me from having to make another trip.

It was unbelievable. Everybody worked their butts off helping us. I never saw it coming, and it just confirmed what I had hoped for when we decided to move. There was no question that we were in the right place.

And where was my good friend Cam? Well, wasn't she just the smartest one of the bunch. She was at the beach. Missed all that work and had a great excuse at the same time. I still wonder if that trip was scheduled before or after I told her when we were moving. Hmmmmm??? That's okay, she would have her work cut out for her later.

Chapter Twenty-Three

Y ou know how when you anticipate something for so long and then when it's over how the letdown can just seem so sad. That's how I felt when everyone went home after our move-in weekend. It was just David and me and a whole hell of a lot of boxes left to unpack. Granted, everybody had pulled triple duty to get us situated on the first floor, but the second floor was all me. And our two car garage was filled to capacity with empty boxes, so even if I got all crazy and busy, I was out of room.

Like I said earlier, our moving company was fabulous. So I called them to see if they had any ideas on what I could do with the boxes. Breaking them down to put out for curbside pick-up was out of the question. They said they'd send a truck over to pick them up. Are you kidding me? And they didn't charge me anything. Well thank you very much. No excuses now. I guess I'd have to get going.

Now here's the weird thing, we had just moved into the house and David had never seen the upstairs. He kept asking if I could help him up there and I kept putting him off. It is one steep staircase and it terrified me to think of both of us taking a header down those stairs. But, can you even imagine living in a house that you hadn't even seen the whole thing?

That was just one of the weird things. As I said, I was on a mission to keep the fear and terror at bay, but I'm here to tell you that you might as well acknowledge it and deal with it, because it's coming out one way or another. I discovered, much to my surprise, that during times of intensely acute stress, I walked and talked (or maybe I should say screamed) in my sleep.

It was creepy. One morning shortly after the move, I woke up and there was an outfit spread out at the end of the bed. I knew those clothes had been in a chest of drawers upstairs, but had absolutely no recollection of climbing the stairs, coming back down and getting back into bed. David did.

"What were you doing last night?" he asked.

"I have no idea," I answered, because I didn't have any memory of it.

Another morning, David said, "Why were you so upset at me last night?"

"I don't think I was. Why?" I said, feeling puzzled by the question.

"You were screaming at me," he said.

"What was I saying?" I said, getting concerned. This was borderline crazy, okay maybe not borderline.

"I'm not sure, you weren't making much sense."

"I think I was walking in my sleep again," I said.

One night I did wake myself up. Unfortunately, I was going out the front door. Thank God I woke up. I just chalked it all up to being tired and having so much to do. Another not so great decision. In other words, I wasn't dealing with all the stress, and I kept putting it off and it wasn't going away. In fact, it was getting worse on some levels.

Within weeks of moving in, David's abilities really started to deteriorate. Poor guy, by 10:00 at night I was so dog tired all I wanted to do was just crawl in bed. He had always been a night person and was so not interested in going to bed. So we rigged up the couch with pillows so that when he sat down he didn't sink so low that he couldn't pull himself up with his walker. It kept him positioned higher so that gravity worked with him. Well that worked for about two days.

I woke up about 1:00 am and David wasn't in bed. Oh crap, I thought to myself. This isn't going to be good.

I ran into the living room and there he lay on the floor, perpendicular to the position where he would have naturally fallen. How did that happen?

"Oh my God, are you okay?" I asked frantically.

"Is anything broken, do you need an ambulance?"

"No, I just hit my head on the wall and I think it bled a little, but I'm okay."

There are no words to describe the profound sadness and despair you feel when you see your once strong husband lying so helplessly on the floor and you know there's no way in hell you can get him up by yourself. There was a small indented spot on the wall where he fell. I couldn't stand it.

That brought the first of a number of phone calls to the Fire Department. I'd call 911 and tell them what was going on and that we didn't need an ambulance; I just needed help lifting him off the floor.

Now I've always had the utmost respect and admiration for firemen, policemen and all the people who put their lives on the line for us every day. But the level of compassion these people showed us was unparalleled. Fortunately for us there was a fire station (No. 14, lucky 14) right around the corner from us. After they got there and had gotten David up, checked his head and calmed me down, I had to take a moment to make sure it wasn't out of bounds to call them with this type of "pseudo-emergency."

"I'm so sorry I had to call you. Is there another number that would be better than 911?" I asked the guy who seemed to be in charge. "I know you have more important things to do," I said.

"No, don't ever hesitate to call us. This is part of what we do," he said with total kindness.

As I said, this was the first of any number of calls I would have to make to them. And okay, I'll admit, I told David after the first couple of times that he better watch out.

"Whoa, David. Those guys are hot," I laughed. "Wouldn't it be awful for me to just give you a nudge to get them over here?"

"Not funny," he answered, but in fact he was laughing.

"I'll make sure it's on the carpet," I continued.

"There is something very wrong with you," he said, shaking his head.

But, we were beginning to adjust to our new life. I finally plowed through all the boxes upstairs and got my office organized, and in the process, completely filled up my garage again with boxes. That moving company came back again. Unbelievable. Still didn't charge me for it. Wow. Dad built me bookcases (from a kit, lest you think he's pulling off woodworking feats) and I created a haven where I could work, work-out and just have a little space. Dad even brought his camera and took pictures so David could see the upstairs. We'd all decided that getting him up and down the stairs was just too dangerous.

I was starting to calm down a little and the sleepwalking and talking stopped – at least for the time being. I called a guy my realtor recommended and he came in and put grab bars in all the places we needed in the bathroom. He put in a banister to the sunporch so David could enjoy that space. It was only three steps but they were doozies. We were making it our own and it felt great.

The most expensive fence in America was completed. We call it the Taj Mafence. Yeah, the homeowners association approved it because we had to match what was already in the neighborhood. Whoever originally decided on the style we had to adhere to had some kind of expensive taste. The doggies now had their own space and they were loving their freedom. Since we'd always had a fenced yard, that leash thing hadn't worked so well with them. The fence created a sort of courtyard effect, where David could go and have privacy and outside time.

It was quickly feeling like home. We all had our space and we had each other and it sort of felt like we were, on some level, trying to create a fortress to keep out all the scariness and the badness that always seemed to be right around the corner. It felt safe and secure. If only there was some way to really keep it all away. But at least for the time being, we had an illusion of normalcy and as I was slowly learning – take what you can get while you can.

Chapter Twenty-Four

Over the next couple of months it became increasingly clear that I was going to need help with David. ALS is much like a long, slow train wreck. It's like a never-ending period of grief, punctuated by periods of energy, fun and hope. I was decidedly not in a state of high energy and wasn't even sure what I needed or where to look for help.

I had used a service to help me get David back and forth to clinic, but really didn't find someone that I thought would be a good match for the long term. All very nice people, but nobody that I sensed David would be comfortable with for any period of time. After all, the things I was starting to really need help with were bathing, changing and those very personal tasks. I just wasn't strong enough physically to feel comfortable not letting him fall or catching him if he did.

As always though, my outlook was for the most part pretty upbeat at least on the surface. It just seemed like I was going to have to behave my way through this whole thing, because not only did my moods affect David, but often times everybody else around me. For whatever reason, I just felt like it was my responsibility to do this with head up and smile on.

So I called Judy, the purveyor of all contacts – real estate, handy men, and hopefully caregivers.

"Hey, I'm hitting the wall here and I'm not sure what to do," I said to her.

Having a daughter with MS, Judy truly knew what I was going through and how difficult it was, not just emotionally, but physically. Her daughter was full grown and Judy was a pip squeak of a woman so the whole thing was very clear to her.

"You ought to call the group home where Kelly is. The director's name is Felicia and she might know somebody," she said.

"I'll call her first just to give her a heads up and she might even just do it herself. You'd love her," she continued.

It might sound like I was making all kinds of unilateral decisions, but David was involved in every single one of them. I might have "encouraged" changes before he was really ready, but we ultimately reached all the decisions together. His only caveat about hiring a caregiver was that it couldn't be a man. Okay, that might be another book for another time, but I respected his wishes and Felicia or somebody she might recommend could be the answer.

Later that afternoon I called and talked to her. I told her our story and how I just needed somebody two or three times a week to help with showers and that kind of stuff. I was still getting him in and out of bed and the rest of it all, but if she could take some of it off me it would go a long way.

Felicia was very low-key and pleasant on the phone and said she'd be interested in doing it herself. Hallelujah! We arranged a time for her to come over and meet us later that week.

I saw her car come in the driveway and went to the front door to meet her. I knew when she stepped out with her bright smile, dreadlocks and friendly demeanor, we had probably just hit the jackpot and found an angel. Turns out, I was oh, so right!

We chatted with her about her background and all those other interview things. Towards the end of our visit, she mentioned that she had gone to Clemson. Deal sealed. She and David formed an instant bond. Thank you God, thank you God, thank you. She was perfect.

After she left I could sense David's relief. The tension had lightened in his face and I could tell he was thinking that this might not be so bad after all. I think he was starting to get the fact that if I could get some kind of break from some things, I might not be so tense myself all the time. And I know how tense I was. Tense and tired.

Felicia started the next week and we just kind of worked out a routine and figured out how this would work. I'd said it before about this whole thing with ALS, but figuring out all this stuff is pretty much like building a plane in the air. It was nice to have another pilot on board.

———————

By January, it had become pretty apparent that David was going to need to move into a wheelchair soon. The firemen knew us by name. I lived on a full adrenaline rush, wondering when the next catastrophe was going to happen. Again, I sort of had to present it gently and sort of maneuver him into thinking it was mostly his idea.

When we visited the clinic that month, we brought it up with the physical therapist, Amber. She agreed and we got things rolling, no pun intended. Unbeknownst to us, getting fitted for a custom wheelchair is not a small thing. There were all kinds of measurements, decisions on styles, seat types, you name it, it was complicated.

But what wasn't complicated was the fact that this would take several months and in the meantime they would just lend us a power chair at no cost. It was a monumental gift to have that level of security coming in days, not months and they would take care of getting it delivered to our house.

Which now brought up the issue of getting a ramp installed. Yet another "where do I start" job for me to figure out. So of course the first place I started was with social worker Amy at the ALS center, who knew everything that Judy didn't and probably more. She steered me to a group from Hickory Grove Baptist Church who had a ministry called "Hearts and Hammers." She called them to get us cleared and then they called me to get us on the schedule.

In the meantime, Mike, the guy who was delivering the chair from the equipment place just used a portable ramp to get the monster into the house. Dear God, that chair was intimidating. But just like with the rolling walker, the dogs had no reaction. They just knew to stay out of the way.

Ironically, I'm pretty sure I was having a bigger reaction than they were. Instead of it symbolizing security and safety for David, it felt like a gigantic neon sign in the room screaming loss, loss, loss. It was like a big, ugly piece of furniture that had no place in your lovely living room, much less your life, anybody's life.

David, on the other hand was pretty cool with the whole thing. Being such a guy, he had no learning curve when it came to using the joy stick control.

He told me, "It's just like driving a boat backwards."

Whatever. I can't drive a boat either.

He and Mike worked to make the adjustments that David would need to get around. I was concerned that it wouldn't fit through the doors, but it did. It turned on a dime and getting in and out of the bathroom didn't present any problems either. This was good. I was starting to see how this could help us both. David would adapt and so would I. We always did.

The Hearts and Hammers guys came a couple of weeks later and within a long weekend they build the mac daddy of ramps in our garage. They build it to code and they built it with love and kindness and good humor.

When they finished, they asked if David could come out and down the ramp for a picture and a prayer. Uh oh, I thought. David was kind of not so much into that "sharing religion" thing.

"David, these guys want you to come out and have a prayer with them. They built this thing in three days, they're only charging us the cost of lumber plus any donation we want to make, so hear this, and hear it clearly, you will go out and pray and you will like it. Got it?" I said with pretty much attitude.

"I'd be happy to," he said graciously.

And he did, and he thanked them for all the work and I felt bad for thinking he wouldn't play nice, because he was genuinely touched by their hard work and help. Because of them, he had the freedom to come in and out as he wanted, safely and securely. That was the biggest gift of all. Just a tad of independence and freedom. Something we all take so for granted. Then I really felt bad. Wasn't the first time, wouldn't be the last.

Chapter Twenty-Five

The *new* normal. That's what we called it whenever we had to make some kind of adjustment to accommodate whatever change was going on with David. I'm pretty sure we were on about our fiftieth *new* normal. Everything was different, yet the same in a lot of ways too. It was a weird existence. While we obviously loved each other, to say this type of situation can challenge a relationship is a massive understatement.

At this point, even with Felicia's help, I was still driving the bus. David needed help with virtually everything. He had minimal use of his arms and while he could still drive his chair once we positioned his hand on the joy stick, that was pretty much the extent of his abilities with his upper body. Fortunately he was still able to chew and swallow, which can be one of the first things to go with ALS patients.

So it was all about the food. I've never minded cooking and since that was one of the few things David could still fully enjoy, I cooked my brains out. And believe me, he wasn't missing a meal. And not only did I cook for him I had to feed him as well. For a while we had a routine that was pretty much working. But after months of cooking and feeding and more cooking and feeding, I thought I would lose my mind.

Cam and I did have regular standing lunch once a week, but it just wasn't enough. Sorry if it sounds selfish and petty, but in the months we'd been there I could count on one hand the number of times I had gone out to dinner at a restaurant and I was just sick to death of the forced closeness that permeated our life. It wasn't anybody's fault, it was just a fact. And I'm sure David was sicker of it than anybody else.

We had supplemented the help we were getting with Felicia by adding another woman, Carolyn, who came in the morning and at bedtime every other weekend. She was also a Godsend and one of the funniest people I knew, even if she didn't know it herself.

For instance, one morning she came in and I had just seen this story on the news about monkeys that were trained to help disabled people. Yeah, you read that right, monkeys.

"Did you see that story on the news about the monkeys helping disabled people?" I asked her.

She was a news junkie, always checking to see who'd gotten shot overnight and had it happened in her neighborhood, which was very near mine, so maybe I should have been paying attention too.

"No," she answered with a funny look on her face.

So I explained that these monkeys could do everything from getting food out of the fridge to heating it in a microwave and serving it to the person and how blown away I was.

"Well, you know what they say," she said, completely serious.

"Uh, uh, what?" I answered. Where was this going? I wasn't trying to replace her with a monkey.

"Those monkeys, they'll turn on you," she declared.

Under our circumstances, this was one of the funniest things I'd heard in months. And, I swear, she had no idea how hilarious it was. But, we loved her and she and David were good together.

Yet, all the while, even though we had some help, it was still pretty much on me. It's hard to know what was going on in David's head because he had zero interest in talking about his "feelings."

I think on some level we both lived in a state of denial about what the future held, because it was just too big to cope with otherwise. But, there were signs that he needed to exert some control over things.

One of those signs was what I'll call the "Horn Incident." Carolyn came one night to help get David in bed and he refused.

"I'm going to stay in my chair," he said.

I could tell by the look on his face that he was going to be a pill about this.

"David, you'll be miserable and uncomfortable. You're already in here so just let us put you to bed. I'm tired and I just need for you to cooperate," I said impatiently.

"No, I'm sleeping in my chair," he said.

"Fine, whatever," I said angrily. "Don't wake me up when you get cold."

So Carolyn left, I got him a blanket and went to bed.

I don't know, it must have been about two or three a.m. and he started telling me to rearrange his blanket.

"No, I'm not getting up. I told you not to wake me up." I was not happy because this whole thing had been utterly predictable.

The controls on his joystick included a horn and he decided that if he wasn't going to sleep, neither was I. He started blowing that horn. Over and over until I swear I thought I could actually kill him. It was beyond obnoxious. So I got up and went upstairs and slept up there. Wow, could we be acting any more immature? I don't think so.

Then there was the "Afrin Incident." Unfortunately, my parents got to enjoy that meltdown. Aside from that pesky ALS, David really didn't have other ailments luckily, but he had caught a cold and believe me I was incredibly sympathetic since I'd had it too and he probably got it from me. Unavoidable.

At the first sign he had caught something I had taken him to see his internist who loaded him up with drugs with the goal of nipping it in the bud and avoiding something more serious like pneumonia. One of the things he had been using was Afrin nose spray which according to the directions shouldn't be more than three days in a row to avoid making your symptoms worse. His doctor told him that after Saturday he should lay off of it for a few days.

So Saturday came and we were in the bathroom and he said he wanted the Afrin.

"No darling, we've got to wait until at least Monday so you won't have worse problems," I said, knowing that this was going to go bad.

He literally started screaming at me, which even as maddening as it was, was understandable. For God's sake, he couldn't even blow his own nose, which is just wrong on so many levels. I just walked out and he followed me.

Mom and Dad were there for the weekend and there was no way they missed that exchange. I told them what was going on as he came in the kitchen.

"David, you're just going to have to understand that you really need to stay off it for a day or two or it won't even work," my dad explained.

And David went off on him. And I mean went off. Well since that had NEVER happened in the entire time they had known him, to say we were shocked doesn't even suffice. Dad just walked out into the garage and didn't say another word. I followed him, leaving David inside with Mom. Wow, did she draw the short straw on that or what?

"Sorry," I said, knowing he knew it wasn't anybody's fault. He just hadn't witnessed first-hand the pent up fury that David obviously had and didn't know how to vent.

We just stood out there and watched it rain. Then there came a peal of laughter from David. We walked in to see what was going on. Mom explained, "I pulled up a stool and sat by David and told him if he didn't cool off about the Afrin I was going to stay right there and keep talking to him." Seems David knew he could only lose if that happened. So he "surrendered".

Now, I tell you those couple of stories not to make David out as the bad guy, but to sort of explain what led up to this next part. Believe me, I'm sure I could come up with fifty examples of my bad behavior too. No, these aren't excuses, just illustrations of what life was like at that point. We were both scared and mad and didn't have any idea what to do about it.

It was another Friday night and like night after night, it seemed like we would get David into bed and he'd start complaining about something or just generally harping at me. I don't know what was different about that night than any of the others, but I snapped. I hit the wall. I was like a crazed maniac, screaming at him, saying awful things. And all the while I was grabbing pills from every bottle I could find, and chasing them down with big gulps of wine. I thought I would break into a million pieces and never put myself back together again. It was horrible. For both of us.

I remember leaving a note on the back door telling Carolyn to come on in and leaving the door unlocked for her. I lay down on the couch and that pretty much sums up what I remember until I woke up in the hospital sometime late the next day.

Crap. I've done it now. That's what went through my head as I got my bearings. My parents were there and Cam and Felicia, Alicia and David. This was just dandy. And oh my God, did I feel like crap.

You know I could go through all kinds of details about what we all now refer to as "the weekend of my discontent," but the point is that I had been silently screaming for help and the scream had finally gotten out. In a big way. I couldn't do it alone and gut it out anymore. I had to have help, physically and more importantly emotionally. Without a doubt, there were probably a lot more productive ways to ask for help, but I've pretty much never done anything the easy way.

A few days later at a follow-up appointment, my internist gave me the names of a couple of psychiatrists and counselors. That's when Linda entered the picture. Lucky me. Linda, a psychologist, would become one of the most important members of Team Sharon. And I now realized that I did need a team.

And Felicia, already a team player, took on an even greater role. She was basically full-time with us from that point on. She and Carolyn. And me. And Mom and Dad, and Cam, and everybody else who cut me slack for doing something so colossally stupid, but that at the time seemed so colossally unavoidable in my mind, became my team. I would get through this with these people who jumped into a situation that many had already run from. It was going to be okay.

Chapter Twenty-Six

Over the next few months we all developed a sort of rhythm. Felicia and Carolyn worked out their schedule for the weekends, making sure I was always covered. Felicia also started handling David's lunch a couple of days a week, which was utter bliss for me to get away from it a little. And just having Felicia around was like getting a warm hug every day. She had quickly become not just my right-hand gal, she was like a sister to me. But it still felt like I had an intense amount of responsibility and there were days I felt like I was being smothered.

Enter Janell. Boy is it true that God puts people in your life when you need them most. Janell was originally from Durham and our family had known her family it seemed like forever. Her parents owned a cleaning business and had cleaned for my parents for years. But, they were really more like extended family. They house-sat and stayed with the dogs when my parents traveled. Their daughters, Yedda and Janell, joined them as they grew older. I knew Janell the least. She came into the picture after I'd already left home.

So you can imagine my surprise when my parents said she was getting married and moving to Charlotte. My wheels started turning. This could be good. I don't remember who got in touch with whom, but shortly after she moved here we chatted. I already had a plan. My idea was to add her to our mix of angels and let her help out with some of David's lunches on the days Felicia wasn't here. But, I had no idea where she was living and the way Charlotte is spread out, she could easily be 45 minutes away from us.

"Hey, welcome to Charlotte," I said to her when we talked.

"I'm not sure what you're doing job-wise, but I've got a proposition for you," I continued.

Well she was interested. And I was ecstatic, because aside from the fact that she's hilarious, she's one of the most reliable, dependable and responsible people I knew. Her whole family is. And believe me when I tell you that to find a third person to supplement Felicia and Carolyn was almost too good to be true.

"So where are you guys living.?," I asked, dreading that she'd say somewhere like Weddington or somewhere else that was virtually in South Carolina.

"We're living right off Sharon Amity in a townhouse," she answered.

You've got to be kidding me. She was living less than a mile from us. This could work. I was doing the happy dance. So we arranged a time for her to come over and get the lay of the land. David was happy too, since it meant one less meal that I was shoving in his mouth. He could eat in peace.

So she started coming and she and Felicia met and once again, just like with Carolyn, if they had conflicts in their schedules they worked it out among themselves, taking one more thing off my plate. Not having to micromanage these wonderful women was truly a gift.

And David adored Janell. She has a wickedly twisted sense of humor, as did David. They would typically watch the news while he had lunch and the sicker the story, the harder the two of them laughed. I would just shake my head.

There was the news story about the guy who bought the contents of a storage unit that hadn't been paid for, so they just sold the stuff. Imagine the buyer's surprise when he opened a grill that was in it and found a hand. A real hand. And then the guy who originally owned the stuff heard about it and wanted his hand back. The story goes on, but the point is that Janell and David thought that was the funniest story on the planet. How David didn't choke to death at some point is still a mystery to me.

Another time a story came on about these tiger cubs.

"Awww, I've always wanted to pet a cub like that," Janell said in all seriousness or so I thought.

"Hey, David, here's an idea," she said. "Have you aged out of that Make A Wish thing?"

We both fell apart. It was so inappropriate, yet so perfectly appropriate and their relationship was cemented. She got it. She never took things too seriously. She never walked on eggshells around him and what she gave him, which Felicia and Carolyn did as well, was his dignity. He was a man, maybe a dying man, but a man nonetheless, who was still part of our world.

Weirdly, around this same time Cam's nanny sort of went off the deep end. It was really sad that somebody her girls really loved just hit the wall with depression and was just not able to handle the stress of two toddlers.

Janell is either a glutton for punishment, or truly the kindest person ever.

"You know, if Cam needs some help I've been a nanny for a couple of people and I'd be glad to do it," she volunteered one day.

Hmmmmmm. This could be good. Good nannies aren't a dime a dozen and Cam was really just looking for someone for a few days a week. So I told Cam about her and told her I'd bring Janell over to meet her and the girls. It was love at first sight on all parts. This was soooooo great. David and I had her help and friendship, Cam had her help and friendship and Janell had a new job and new friends in her new town. I think they call it synchronicity or put another way – everybody plays, everybody wins.

The irony of this situation was that Cam and I talked a lot about how in many, many ways we were living in a kind of parallel universe. So having Janell in both our lives just fit. I in no way mean to sound unkind, but dealing with David and his illness mirrored Cam's challenges with her two young girls.

David's frustrations with his inability to do much of anything took on the characteristics of a toddler's tantrum. The constant needs they had that we were responsible for meeting were so similar. It was such a gigantic responsibility and while some days it felt so rewarding, other days felt awful and exhausting. Their pain was our pain and their joy was our joy.

It was unbelievable to me that while we were at such distinctly different points in our lives, on another level we were in exactly the same place. And there's nothing my misery loved more than a little company.

So things were progressing in an okay way and I was starting to create some kind of life for myself that didn't exclude David, but gave me a little sense of my own independence and freedom. With David's lunch covered on most weekdays, I joined Curves, not necessarily to get into shape, but more to get out of the house. I'm not much of a shopper, so cruising the malls to kill time had zero appeal. Curves was close and it seemed like a good idea. And it was, I met Menge.

You know how there are just some people that the chemistry is just immediate. We started chatting while we exercised and it was like I'd known her forever. It was just so easy. I think at a certain age, making new friends is just difficult. Filling in the back story so they know who you are and where you came from all just seemed daunting. It wasn't that way with Menge, the blanks sort of just filled themselves in. I found myself laughing – a lot. Much like with Cam. It was just no pressure, no hassle.

We just naturally fell into a routine of lunches and the occasional dinners and I actually began to start feeling like I could figure this whole "new life" thing out. I know that I was better with David. Less stressed, less tense. It was generally a much kinder atmosphere at our house these days. Hey maybe they're on to something with this exercise thing. It does help stress. Hmmmmmm. Who knew? And having a new friend to share it with made it actually seem like fun.

So even though we'd been through a very rough patch, the pieces were coming together and while the team was growing, it was quality, not quantity that mattered. How did I get so lucky to have found three of the kindest people on the planet? I think that's where a "Thank you God" comes in.

Chapter Twenty-Seven

Life moved along relatively smoothly. We settled into our routine and I even started to take a weekend here and there to visit my parents or my brother Chuck and his family in Iowa. Man, you really know you need a break when your destination of choice is Iowa. In winter. But the visits to them were like a shot of energy. Who cares if the high is five degrees?

One of the first trips I took out to Iowa to see them was the second week in December. My parents had made it an annual trip to celebrate my nephew Charlie's birthday, which is the 21st and to do an early Christmas with their family. I decided this year I would join them.

I'm pretty sure that I should have seen a screaming red flag when my brother called.

"Hey, we're so glad you're coming out. Just wanted to let you know to bring some *very* warm clothes," he laughed.

I thought he was just talking about it being cold and at the time didn't think too much of it. My bad. Thankfully I did pack warm stuff because unbeknownst to me we were all going to be in the Cedar Rapids Christmas Parade. Yeah, I know. Who would've seen that coming?

Chuck owns a manufacturing company called Raining Rose. They make lip balm, lotions, soaps and other assorted products. He, his family and all his employees, plus Mom and Dad, me and their two Irish Wolfhounds were going to march behind his logoed company car down Main Street.

Before all this had happened with David and me there wasn't a chance in hell that I would've been game for marching in the freezing cold in a freaking parade. But, things were shifting in so many ways for me that I thought "why not?"

It was a riot. My sister-in-law filled a thermos with wine for us. "Mother's little helper," she laughed.

We all piled into the car and drove over to Raining Rose to walk over to the staging area for the parade. And please understand, I'm using the word "parade" very loosely here. It was like a rag tag group of people who had somehow blundered into a wobbly line walking down Main Street. It was hilarious. And it was snowing by the time we got going. I mean really, really snowing.

Since Raining Rose makes lip balm, we all had baskets full of samples to toss out to the crowd. What we found out later was that because it was so stinking cold the poor people in the crowd felt like they were being pelted with rocks every time we'd throw them. Oops. But it was fun. And the wine didn't hurt the cause either.

It was the first of many trips I would take to visit them and not only did I find myself reenergized when I got home, a fringe benefit was a newfound relationship with my niece and nephews. Lucky me.

David was finding his way as well. He and Felicia had their routine and every ten days or so would go on one of their "outings." We called it "driving Mr. Davey." It was great. Felicia would load him into the car and they would set out for places like Costco, or Home Depot or Myers Park Hardware. Or sometimes they would just drive around.

I had a couple of hours with the house all to myself, which seemed like pure bliss. I could just chill. Be off duty so to speak and not driving around trying to manufacture something to do. I had never realized how much I cherished a little time alone until the circumstances forced our constant togetherness. We both got a much needed break and it was making life seem a little more bearable.

Our patio never looked better than that spring. They came home with all kinds of crazy plants and pots and bushes and hanging baskets. David supervised, while Felicia did the planting, potting and watering. He developed a thing for succulent plants. Whatever tripped his trigger was my feeling about that. David basked in the sun on our patio, which because it's fenced in, is very courtyard-like and private. It became his haven. No prying eyes of neighbors. No traffic noise. Just a little place of peace for him. Felicia just sitting quietly, never needing to force a conversation or fill in the lulls. It was lovely to watch their friendship deepen and their bond get stronger and stronger. It was such a gift to me to know that in Felicia, I had found another person who understood David almost as well as I did, and as a result, cared for him in a way that was unmatched.

In retrospect, I realize now how much David listened to me. If I mentioned that our grill brush was worn out, in they'd come in with the mac daddy of grill utensils. If I said my office was hot upstairs, voila, new fans. My knives were old and dull, tah dah, a new set of Henkel knives in their own handy block. Granted, his outing weren't always purely selfless. Aside from the plants, there was usually a giant cheesecake involved – his favorite. Or some other treat that he found. Good for him.

These outings weren't just a way for David to maintain some semblance of independence, it was his way of contributing to the household needs, and to our relationship as well. Oh, the myopia of caregiving. Too busy, too tired, too caught up thinking three steps ahead to the next crisis.

At the time, I certainly appreciated his efforts, but it just didn't sink in how truly meaningful this was. I was often too involved in the business and chores of daily living and didn't necessarily take the time to really think about the bigger picture. I think that's a hazard that many caregivers encounter – you kind of can't see the forest for the trees. It's a lesson I wish I had learned earlier rather than later.

So I guess we were sort of starting to learn how to take care of ourselves and each other in a new way. The whole concept of caregiving was so alien to me. I just wasn't a nurturer by nature. I constantly battled the myriad emotions that went along with the whole caregiving thing -- guilt, resentment, love, empathy, anger, fear, fleeting moments of joy – it was a crazy maze of feelings that required daily navigation.

In all honesty, I don't think there's anyone on the planet who says "hey, sign me up for this." Except of course, Felicia, Carolyn and Janell – Lord love 'em. I think most people are probably more like me. You sort of get shoved into the role and you have absolutely no idea what you're doing. It's insane on so many levels. I mean, my God, you love this person and want nothing but the best for them, but at the same time you get so sick of them and their needs. It's a pendulum, that when it's not swinging wildly from side to side, it's stuck in the middle banging you in the head with its constancy. And it's lonely. Sure I had friends, family and David, but I was living in a constant state of fight or flight. You never really ramp your adrenaline down when you feel such total responsibility for another person.

When I think about that time now, I can appreciate the simplicity of what made each of us happy. It wasn't the big salary, or the big house or the cool car. It was those days that were peaceful. It was time spent soaking up the warm sunlight. It was time together where we just loved each other and didn't let our fear get in the way of a perfect spring day. It was laughing at our silly dogs trying to drink from the hose.

Those days when we just stayed in the moment were our best. We weren't looking back. We weren't looking forward. We were just right there with each other. Like I said, it's a lesson I wished I had learned sooner rather than later.

Chapter Twenty-Eight

The one thing I know for certain about ALS is that it doesn't progress in an orderly fashion. While some people with the disease succumb in a matter of months, others hang on for years. What I also know is that this awful disease has the capacity to lull you into an utterly false sense of stability. Time sort of loses meaning. Days become weeks and months and years. There is no predicting when the next downhill slide will come, or the next loss of what little abilities are left. Since no one, doctors, caregivers or even the patient, has any idea what is around the corner, you are almost lulled into a false sense of security. As you're constantly adapting to whatever the new normal is, it seems like it actually is normal – at least from the inside.

Over the next few months we were living in a very delicately balanced world. Everybody had their routines and nothing seemed imminent. I had become weirdly rigid about maintaining what order I could. The routine was key to our sanity. David's days were infinitely easier when the schedule was adhered to. I guess we were both trying to control the uncontrollable. But, like it always did, the situation changed.

I realized at some point that Felicia was working for us about 26 days out of 30 every month. She wasn't here all day, but she was definitely here every morning, at bedtime and three or four hours a few days a week. That might not seem like that much on the surface, but do you know how much it disrupts someone's life to get in their car every night at 10:30 or 11:00 to come to work for a half hour? She never complained or seemed put out, but I would have had to be an idiot not to acknowledge the sacrifices she made for us.

Carolyn was here every other weekend to help David get up in the morning and get into bed at night, but she couldn't take on more time because she had a full time job working at a group home for disabled women. How on earth was I able to find these saints I asked myself over and over again.

So I started trying to find more help. Easier said than done.

I started by calling one of the home healthcare agencies to see if we could find someone through them. My goal was to initially get somebody just to help with feeding David his supper. If they had good rapport and fit in, then maybe we could train them for the more "hands on" task of helping transfer him in and out of bed, dressing, etc. Enter Janet.

Janet was older than I had anticipated, but the agency said she was highly qualified. Okay, so I'm pretty sure now that we had very different definitions of "highly qualified." The agency had touted their services as including hands on patient care and light housekeeping, cooking, etc.

Her first day was fine. She was kind of quiet, but that wasn't so bad since David wasn't exactly chatty. She helped with his dinner and went on her way. Not exactly back breaking work.

The next night she showed up and quit. I guess asking her to clean the kitchen after our dinner (which, by the way, I had offered for her to join us) was out of bounds. I was pissed. She told me she had already called the agency, yet her supervisor hadn't had the courtesy to call me.

So the next day I called them back to see what was what.

"Janet quit, you didn't call me and now I'm back at square one," I told Rudy, her supervisor.

Well Rudy was very, very apologetic and said he had talked to our case nurse and they had the perfect replacement. She had worked with an ALS patient before and would be a great match – young, lively and full of personality.

I know now that this description is much like all the euphemisms they use in real estate. Their ads describe a house as a cute, fixer-upper when what they mean is a small toxic dump.

Gigi was scheduled to come for an interview on a Saturday morning at 11:00. Well 11:00 came and went. Now I really was pissed. This was so damn ridiculous. I'm trying to throw money at these people and I've got a no show?

Well after numerous phone calls to their "staffed 24 hours a day" line I finally got a phone call from Gigi herself. She told me that Rudy had told her 1:00 that afternoon, not 11:00. She could still come if it suited me. Okay, fine. Maybe it was just a miscommunication. Or maybe Rudy was an idiot. I know where I'd put my money.

Gigi finally showed up and she actually was delightful. She did seem young, lively and full of personality. David was okay with her so we planned a schedule that fit in with the four other jobs she seemed to hold down. Wow, I thought, if she's this dependable, this could work.

So she started coming and when I offered her dinner, she was all in.

"That would be great. I have to go to my overnight shift with an Alzheimer's patient and don't really get a chance to eat," she said gratefully.

So now I was cooking pretty much every night for three. Whatever. But initially, it was okay. She was pretty easy to have around and she would pick up dinner for David if I made plans to go out, which wasn't often. I'm not sure Felicia was getting anything out of this, but I was to a degree and if Gigi seemed to keep working out, we might be onto something.

For the next few weeks things were sort of just rolling along. Gigi was dependable, if a little flaky, but generally okay. After a couple of weeks I had poached her from the agency. Do I feel the teensiest bit bad about that? No not even a little. She was the one doing the work, why should I pay the agency twice what they paid her? They didn't do jack for me or David except bill us. We worked out a deal where everybody played and everybody won – except Rudy. Tough.

I hadn't forgotten about Felicia and was putting out feelers to everybody I knew to find somebody to supplement her. With Gigi's other jobs, she couldn't take on more hours right at the moment. I talked to Mom and Dad and they called in every contact they knew in Charlotte and wherever that might know of someone. I was definitely not calling the agency again. We were not having any luck.

Felicia in fact had an idea to try the director at the men's group home that was the counterpart to the home where she had worked when she started with us. I don't remember which one of us got in touch with the director, but he had a guy, ironically, named David, who was interested. The director was willing to cut him some slack on his schedule to do the night shift periodically.

David was scheduled to come for an interview on another Saturday morning. What was wrong with me, did I never learn? But, he did show up, more or less on time. He was a fine strapping guy and he was very pleasant. He would be in and out as soon as David was up in the morning or in bed at night, so his personality was less important. He just needed to be nice and respectful and kind with my David.

He agreed to start the next Saturday morning with Felicia on board to train him. They both showed up and things seemed to go well. My David didn't have any complaints so yea! maybe we had finally found somebody.

That night, oh, sometime around 10:30 the phone rang. It was David.

"Uh, hey, I'm not going to be able to come tonight. I don't have any gas," he said nervously.

Are you freaking kidding me? What exactly do you say to that?

"I'm not going to be able to get gas until I get paid next week, so I won't be there tomorrow either," he continued in response to my silence.

Great, just great. I was livid.

When Felicia got there she was as surprised as I was, but Felicia being the calm in the storm convinced me that he really was highly recommended (do you see a trend here) and that it was probably worth giving him another chance. Okay. I could do that.

Do you want to write this next paragraph?

Yeah, the next weekend, he couldn't make it either. Aaaaarrrgh. I was losing my mind. Believe me when I say that I wasn't underpaying these people either. I was probably paying them twice what they would make somewhere else and I was happy to do so. If they would just show up.

It was all becoming just too much. I was frustrated. David was frustrated at the ongoing parade of imbeciles because it was him they were slinging around like a sack of flour. It was just such an impossible situation. And I didn't have any solutions. For once I was really, really out of answers.

Legend: Hammond/McAlister family
  Front row: Peggy and Charles Hammond
  Rear row: Chuck and Ann Hammond, Sharon and David McAlister
  (all are left to right, circa 2000)

Legend: Chuck and Ann Hammond's children
    From left: Oliver, Charlie and Katie Hammond
    Circa 2002

Legend: Sharon H. McAlister

Legend: David McAlister

Legend: David McAlister and Charles Hammond golfing in Hawaii

Legend: Sharon McAlister and Peggy Hammond

Legend: David several years after being diagnosed with Lou Gehrig's disease (ALS)
    Left to right: Alisha Pryor, Felicia Stevenson, Judy Perrell, David and Sharon
    McAlister
    2 Jack Russell Terriers - Peggy and Betty

Legend: 4 dogs - 2 Jack Russell Terriers and 2 dachshunds

PART II

Charles B. Hammond, M.D.

Chapter Twenty-Nine

In early 2008, when Sharon began writing this book, little did I imagine I would be trying to finish it. She sent us the following e-mail with her first chapter: "Okay, here are the rules. NO editing. NO derogatory comments, and NO suggestions unless I ask. This is my book. Not a collaborative effort, not a book by committee. But I would LOVE all your encouragement and love that you always have for me. I need to do this by myself but with support along the way. Let's let the teacher coach me through this. But, you're part of the story, so I want to share the journey with you. I love you both. Sharon."

As Sharon's dad (and David's "adopted" one), it seems I have been elected to complete this amazing story. A story of pain and loss, but also about love and caring. Peggy, my wife and Sharon's mom, is participating fully – in the hopes of not only helping me, but keeping it on track. Sharon, who described herself as "mini-me", hit the nail on the head – we both loved books, words and writing. Unfortunately, mine centered on medicine and science, - not the flowing prose which came from Sharon. We had short fuses but got over it quite rapidly – we cared deeply for each other, although some would doubt that as our volatility was such that it seemed we could never heal some of our disagreements (particularly during her adolescent years). But we could and did. Later, we regained our closeness, and it was nearly overwhelming to watch how these diseases were ending their physical beings. Fortunately, their personas were still intact. Let me continue their story.

First, I would point out that all Sharon has written was true. There were amazing problems for both of them. What she didn't write about enough was the awesome grace and resiliency of them both. Through breast cancer and ALS each showed their true mettle as they adapted to each "new normal". For Sharon – life threat, disfigurement, multiple therapies, becoming a caregiver and facing the death of her husband; and for David – life threat (which became a promise), loss of independence – movement, speech, lifestyle and the ability to earn a living. As to be expected, there were major stresses and there were times they coped poorly. But also there was love and caring, celebrations of life and their togetherness. Neighbors and friends, new and old, rallied. Truly, "It takes a village", not only in child rearing but also in survival of catastrophic and prolonged illnesses. Peggy and I saw all of this and were awed and grateful for the outpouring from so many individuals. Both Sharon and David encountered so many problems and disappointments, but seemingly someone always emerged to help provide a solution or, at least, to help develop an adaptation.

You have read of Sharon's trials with breast cancer, still more would occur, but for that time it was quiescent. At the time she stopped writing their problems were centered on David's inability to move and to care for himself. Sharon, as well as Felicia, Carolyn and Janell were exhausted and doing all they could do. Appropriate further home care could not be found, at least as far as reliability. Thus, it was time to find the best next adaptation – which Sharon and David agreed would be an inpatient facility near to their home – fully staffed with home-like facilities and personnel with competent and caring attitudes. With her usual energy Sharon set out to find such a facility for "the perfect place". After visits to many places she found Sunrise on Providence Assisted Living which seemed to fit all of their needs.

She and Felicia took David to see it, and he agreed it was suitable and that it was time to make a change. More losses for David – his home, the dogs and the constant interactions with Sharon, Felicia and the others who helped. On the other hand, much of his lifestyle moved with him. His relationship with Sharon seemed to actually improve as he was receiving better care and she was much less fatigued. The visits, cocktail parties and friends continued, including Samantha and Ann (Cam and Jamie's kids) Betty and Peggy (their two Jack Russell Terriers) and many others. David still used his power chair, and he found that not only was a bird feeder in his window, but also a hungry squirrel to provide entertainment. Felicia continued many of her prior efforts – including "driving Mr. Davey" for regular times out. Throughout David's time there Sharon continued to visit him often. It truly removed the pressures of cooking, feeding him, moving him and providing physical care, As expected, there were minor problems such as menus, mix-ups in various meals and so forth – but David and we all felt he was in the best situation possible. The staff was superb and exhibited love and concern as well as competence and compatibility. David lived there for more than a year until his death on June 24, 2008.

We all have wonderful memories of these times and places. My best mental picture is of David sitting in his power chair in the middle of his family room sucking on a straw from his vodka drink held by a kiddie cup holder while many people swirled around him and included him. From children to older adults, all seemed drawn to include him. There would be music and food (although David had to eat earlier) and laughter. Friends, old and new, came often and stayed significant times. It seems that if David couldn't go to these get-togethers, the party came to him. Surely Charlotte was a good place to be for them! These continued, albeit smaller at Sunrise until David's later days.

Speaking of Sunrise, the facility was mainly populated by older people. David, who primarily stayed in his larger room in the power chair, primarily interacted with the staff, outside visitors, Sharon and the TV set – and the squirrel in his window – as his mobility continued to deteriorate. When he could no longer speak, Sharon and David used a speech board, and David could blink as she pointed to letters to spell out what he wanted to say. There were other, electronic options but none David wanted to pursue. Sharon, on the other hand, did meet and mingle with some of the individuals who lived there and became good friends with many of them. Sunrise was no more than 10 minutes from their home, and I truly believe her car could have found its own way.

For some interval after David's more to Sunrise, Sharon arranged for his trips back to their home for short visits and a few overnights and on holidays. Using the excellent Charlotte transport system for the handicapped, David could drive his wheelchair into a van, have it "locked down" and drive it off at home. We were increasingly thankful for the ramp built at their home by the church as this could not have been done without it. Their dogs were ecstatic to see him, as while Sharon had tried repeatedly to bring them for visits, their hyperactivity wouldn't seem to allow it. Sadly, as David continued to deteriorate, these visits had to stop.

Chapter Thirty

During these times Peggy and I spent many days and holidays in Charlotte. I don't seem to be able to just sit and do nothing. So I became the local "gardener" – adding plants, fixing flower beds, planting trees and bushes. When David was still active and the weather was good he would come down the ramp in his power chair and "hang out" with me in the yard. Sharon, a person who cared little about the yard for many years would rarely come out at first – but later she came out and actually worked with me. I recall that we planted hundreds of tulips and other bulbs, flowering trees, vines along the fences and many bushes. I wondered who had taken over Sharon's body and brought to me that new interest and energy. Together, we all found joy in helping to turn their back yard into a much better place for us all to be outdoors and together.

One Christmas while David was ill, someone told Sharon about a little boy whose mom had told him there could be no Christmas at their house. She found him later in his room wrapping up some of his old toys. He told her that he was doing this so that he would have something to open on Christmas. At that point in the story Sharon was on a mission to see that he did have a Christmas. She involved many others. I don't mean a few toys and books. Our assignment was a Play Station which we gladly supplied, and others provided shoes, clothes and many other things. He came to Sharon's home on Christmas Eve and opened all his gifts. What a special Christmas that made for all of us. He was so pleased and so thankful. He said it was the best Christmas he ever had, and Sharon fully agreed.

There are some other good stories about David and Felicia. When David was still able he loved to seek and buy presents for others – Peggy and Sharon especially. Sharon wrote about the things he especially loved to personally get for Peggy. David very badly wanted to buy a sculpture for Sharon. When he couldn't do it himself he enlisted Felicia to help. He found on the web a man in Virginia who made such things and arranged to buy one – then he and Felicia got into a car and met the man half way to transfer it. They brought it back to Charlotte and Felicia set it up in the back yard – a concrete base with a metal spiral on top which rotated in the wind. He was absolutely proud when he presented it to Sharon who loved it. It is now situated in Peggy's and my garden, and we love it as well.

Another example was when David sought and found a print of a dachshund dog by Picasso. Peggy and I have had at least one such dog at all times for nearly 50 years – often two of them. We then had two – Mollie and Muffin – and they usually came to Charlotte when we did. David found the print on line, bought it and gave it to us his last Christmas. It proudly hangs in our home today, a symbol of caring and doing from David.

Through the later years of David's illness, Sharon wrote of her struggles with her mental health and the "finding" of Linda Smith, her psychologist. Linda became her window to a more healthy world and a true friend for her. I only met her at David's memorial service, but we are eternally grateful to her for all she did for Sharon during these very stressful times.

During the flu "epidemic" in 2007, we could not find any source of a flu shot for David as production was then severely limited. A physician friend of mine heard of our problem and simply "showed up" on their doorstep one evening, bringing the flu shot for David. He administered it, then had to depart to other duties. Surely, Dr. Frank Harrison provided an important "house call" – one we will never forget.

Others also did many wonderful things. After David moved to Sunrise his hands had become chronically swollen, and his wedding and college rings were too tight. Sharon called a jeweler she knew to arrange to bring David (a major undertaking now) to get them cut off. The jeweler appeared at Sunrise within an hour of her call and cut them off there – then took them back to his shop, fully repaired them, at no charge, and presented them as a gift to Sharon with the statement that he had had a relative with ALS and simply wanted to do this for them. Sharon wore the wedding band on a chain around her neck for some interval thereafter.

There were so many individuals who did so much for Sharon and David – usually, without any one of us asking. People seemed to know when they were needed and then appeared. We are forever grateful for their humanism and concern.

Chapter Thirty-One

David continued to deteriorate after he moved to Sunrise – losing motion until he was unable to run his power chair at all, although he still sat in it after being moved from bed with a lift. It also required the lift to get him into the bathroom or shower. All of this made it obvious he was now where he needed to be (Sunrise) and no longer at home.

A common problem for persons with ALS is, as the process advances, that the respiratory muscles weaken and this makes breathing profoundly more difficult. Placing a tracheostomy in the neck into the trachea and attaching a ventilator can prolong life for such patients for a significant interval of time. A number of ALS patients decide <u>not</u> to have this done, as did David as he felt it prolonged "existence", not really life. He never faltered in his decision. I think I too would have chosen that option.

One thing David loved during this time was food. Like the ventilator, he rejected the placement of a feeding tube, but Sharon had already moved him to pureed foods, and he was fortunate that he could still swallow small amounts. From early on at home David had Felicia (and later Janell) bringing in things he liked to eat – from Captain D's to barbecue it was a constant parade of foods he loved (I am not necessarily speaking for myself). This continued even after he moved to the assisted living facility. He also loved his vodka and grapefruit juice – and late every afternoon he would have someone fix it and would drink it through a straw from a gadget that held his cup. I must admit we often joined him during these hours. Peace must have come hard to David, but one very rarely saw this show through.

Finally, David began a downhill spiral that ended in his death. Eating and food lost their allure, and breathing became an increasing problem. His muscles were simply giving out from lack of nerve function. Hospice was called in to Sunrise and provided wonderful control and caring during his last few weeks. David died on June 24, 2008, at peace, ending what must have seemed to him an interminable path. Sharon later wrote "David's Day" which describes his death.

David's memorial service was held on July 1, 2008 in Charlotte at the Myers Park Presbyterian Church. The Reverend Joe Harvard, our minister in Durham and the person who married David and Sharon, presided. His wife Carlisle also came to lend support to us all. Joe provided a wonderful homily, "A Whole Life", and a number of David and Sharon's friends came. It was a sad occasion but helped relieve the sorrow we all felt. Afterward, we held a reception at their home that went on until the later hours as we all cried and laughed, remembering good times and bad – but especially remembering David whose loss was so real to us all. I am also including my comments at the service for David, for I believe they describe the man David was and our relationship to each other. We will remember David Warren McAlister forever. May he rest in peace.

David's Day

By Sharon McAlister

A day by most definitions is a 24 hour period, usually beginning and ending at midnight. But other definitions are more appropriate – a time or period of time in the past, present or future. Some days blend into each other, while some days are indelibly etched into your mind from that one beginning moment to a final, inevitable conclusion.

June 23rd, 10:30 am – Not like all the other days had been lately. It felt so different, wondering how David was doing that morning and how bad had it gotten overnight. Was he okay? Was he in pain? Or was he better today – he'd snapped back, relatively speaking – from tough stretches before during this four and a half year battle.

Five and a half years ago I had been diagnosed with Stage 3 Breast Cancer. As unconcerned and glib as I was about my own little journey with cancer, David's situation had proven to be a whole different beast. Call it naiveté, call it ignorance, but it just really didn't occur to me that I was facing anything life threatening. I had no intention whatsoever of dying of that stinking disease. It just seemed wholly inconvenient to me. David's situation went way beyond inconvenient. It was inconceivable. How could this man I loved be dealing with this sort of hellish existence?

June 23rd, 12:00 noon – I don't care what Hospice says about the body providing natural anesthesia as the body shuts down; I just had to take one look to know he was suffering. And his suffering brought me to my knees – literally.

"Oh honey, what can I do?" I said, trying with everything I held dear not to fall apart.

Since he couldn't talk I used the letter board. Haltingly, he used his eyes to spell out H – O – S – P.

"Hospital," I asked.

Twenty plus years together gives you the ability to jump into each other's heads.

One blink which translated to "yes," he answered.

"Oh babe, there's nothing they can do for you at this point. Let me call the nurse and I'll get her to give you some morphine. I thought I would die from the pain of denying him the perceived help he thought might still be possible.

Again, one blink and I could tell he needed to say more. He spelled out T-H-I-R.

"Thirsty," I ventured. One blink.

Since he hadn't had more than a few sips in days I'm sure he was excruciatingly thirsty. My heart was breaking even as his was giving up.

I got as much water in him as he could take, but when you pretty much can't move your lips or swallow, that's a fairly daunting effort.

Again, he needed to tell me more and spelled B-E-D.

"You want to get back into bed?"

This was the same person that had been in a wheelchair for the past three years and never ever given up and gone back to bed.

So I got them to bring the morphine and the care managers got him back into bed. It was hard to believe that it was almost 3:00 in the afternoon. I went home while he rested. I'd see him tomorrow.

For months while I went through my treatment David had been struggling with what had at first appeared to be really difficult allergies. After so many appointments with no improvement he was going to a neurologist. I finally got up the nerve to ask him if he had some idea of what was going on. Never did I see this answer coming.

"I think I have ALS, you know Lou Gehrig's disease," he said so quietly I thought surely I must have misheard him.

An avid reader of mystery and suspense novels, I was a big fan of the author Joy Fielding. So I had pretty much read all of her books. A few years before any of this had happened I stumbled onto one of her books that was decidedly <u>not</u>

her typical fare – The First Time. It was about a woman diagnosed with Lou Gehrig's disease so I had a crystal clear picture of what a diagnosis of ALS would mean to us.

For the uninitiated, ALS stands for Amyotrophic Lateral Sclerosis. ALS is a disease of the parts of the nervous system that control voluntary muscle movement. The clinical description of ALS explains that nerve cells that control muscle cells are gradually lost. As these motor neurons are lost, the muscles they control become weak and then nonfunctional. Eventually, the person with ALS is paralyzed.

But the kicker of this horrific disease is that the vast majority of patients retain all brain function and awareness. Ain't that grand? So you're sitting there not able to move a muscle, often times not even able to talk and you know exactly what's going on. I don't care what the medical profession says ALS stands for – I know what it stands for -- "A Life Shattered."

June 23ʳᵈ, 8:30 pm – I don't know what drove me back over to David that night – guilt, God or gut wrenching love and fear, but I knew I had to get back to him. So I called the friend I always called on the hardest days -- Cam. Now, Cam may be a tiny little sprite of a person, but she has a gargantuan spirit and has carried my Sasquatch self on her back during the toughest of times.

I met her in the lobby and I went into David's room first. They were just getting him into bed and his caregiver Chris was literally <u>in</u> his bed on one side trying to pull him up. So I jumped on the other side and we got him comfortable. It earned me a wink from him. Always a sign of thank you. His once strong and healthy body was so frail and smallish; I just wanted to cradle him and make it all go away.

Cam came in then and we sat with him. He was awake and aware and incredibly peaceful. I really can't even remember exactly what was said, it was just important that it got said -- for all of us.

As we left, I kissed him and told him I loved him and that whatever he needed was okay with me. I guess that was my inept way of saying, "I'll be okay, so you go if you need to."

Cam kissed him on the forehead and squeezed his hands. We walked into the hall and along with Chris stood in a three-way hug and sobbed. He was only 47-years old.

The thing that's important to know about David and me is that we never gave up on fun during his illness. Sure there were tears, frustrations and rage at the hopelessness and helplessness of it all. (Believe me when you yell at somebody confined to a wheelchair it's not your finest moment.) But, there were also lots of laughs, friends and family that were with us through the whole journey. We had tree trimming parties with silly hats, we had cocktail parties where David sipped his vodka and grapefruit juice through a straw in a cup being held up by a kiddy cupholder – Mother's Third Arm was what that silly cupholder was called. We talked about times that were good and we tried to love each other the best way we could. It's all we could do.

June 24th, 9:30 am – I knew I needed to get dressed and get to David, but I felt immobile. Geez, it was June and I had the gas logs turned on – I was just cold and out of ideas of how to help him or myself for that matter. Say a prayer I told myself – over and over I told myself.

The phone rang about 10:15 that morning.

"Sharon, it's Eva," said the nurse we adored from the assisted living facility.

"David has his wings. You have a guardian angel now," she said quietly.

So the day was over and my journey forward began. And for the first time in so many years I felt like David was back beside me, supporting me, and he was finally at peace.

My friend saw an owl as she was leaving our house the night he died and swore it was David, flying free, letting her know he was okay. A few days later as I sat on my neighbor's patio, she pointed to her fence. There sat an owl. Neither of us had ever seen an owl in the neighborhood and I hadn't told her about the first sighting. And the next week another friend who lived in another area of town heard her dogs growling at something on her deck and when she looked out, there sat an owl. She didn't know about either of the first two sightings. Take what you want from that. I know I have.

Tribute to David Warren McAlister

Given at David's Funeral, July 1, 2008
Charles B. Hammond, M.D.

I come today to speak about our "second son", David Warren McAlister, who died on Tuesday, June 24, 2008 at the age of 47. David had struggled with amyotrophic lateral sclerosis (ALS or Lou Gehrig's disease) for the last 5 years.

David was born and grew up in Anderson, SC, not far from Greenville. He then attended Clemson University - an experience that forever made him a football fan (for Clemson, I mean). After graduation he entered the world of sales - and did it exceedingly well. He later lived in Cary and Charlotte, plying his trade. I once asked David how he would pick a product or area for sales.

His answer, a simple one, "Give them the razor, then sell them the blades." He was living and working in sales when he met and ultimately married our daughter, Sharon.

That reminds me of a story about Sharon. She had a special relationship with her grandfather, Peggy's dad, Bill. They often joked with one another. Bill, in his 80's, teased her a lot. One day Sharon said to him, "Granddaddy, you are as old as dirt." After reflecting on his 29-year-old, unmarried granddaughter, he simply replied, "How old do you have to be and be unmarried before they call you an old maid?" Fortunately, Sharon and David were married later that year, before she was 30 - the time Bill felt answered that question.

After their marriage in Durham, Sharon and David moved to Charlotte, then Atlanta, then back to Greenville, SC. They continued working and bought a home and 2 Jack Russell Terriers, Peggy and Betty, named for Sharon's mother and her dear friend, Betty Henderson - their claim to fame!

It was later in 2002 that Sharon was diagnosed with a Stage III advanced breast cancer - she was vigorously treated and, thankfully, is now well - more than 5 years later. Then, two months after the end of her treatment, one day before his 43rd birthday, David was diagnosed with ALS.

David struggled with ALS as it inexorably shut down his muscles. Lost was his ability to drive, walk, talk, and finally his ability to move at all. They had a home in Greenville, SC - unfortunately, with their bedroom upstairs, lots of steps and a steep slope in the yard. They moved to Charlotte, bought another, better-suited home, and to be closer to the only ALS Center in the Southeast. David's disease steadily advanced, and about a year ago it became obvious that he could not be cared for at home any longer - he moved to Sunrise Assisted Living about 4 miles from their home. There he did well though the disease continued to progress until he was totally paralyzed. About 10 days before he died, hospice entered the picture, and he died peacefully one week ago. Throughout it all he was surrounded by family, friends and neighbors who cared for him.

There are many people who cared for and about David. First, and most importantly, his wife - our daughter - Sharon. She gave and gave to the very end - first at home, lifting and feeding and much more, and later - doing much of the same at Sunrise. Day in and day out, no quarter asked, she did the job with love and caring. I never doubted Sharon's will - but we will forever be impressed with the depth of her love and commitment - starting only 2 months after finishing her own treatment. Sharon, I salute you!

Throughout all of this we can only be grateful for caring friends and caregivers. First and foremost - Felicia Stevenson. Felicia, you were so much more than a "careperson". You have our eternal gratitude for becoming a member of our family, to us and to David. For food you brought in, to rides for David in the community, and for the loving care and so much more that you showed to David and Sharon, we thank you and Alisha Pryor as well. Carolyn Wallace also helped days and nights. Thank you, Carolyn. The staff at Sunrise were loving, efficient and provided excellent care for more than a year. The staff at the ALS Center were experienced and capable, but more importantly, they cared.

ALS is a disease without a cure yet - the ALS Center was a place of hope and caring. Much more, they help patients live with this horrible disease with hope through clinical trials and help them to adapt to living functionally with the ravages of this disease.

Also, thanks to friends - to Janell Johnson (and her husband, Wynn), who moved to Charlotte from Durham after their marriage, and she became his "eating buddy". Every Friday she asked what he wanted for lunch, got it, and they shared it. The most amazing array of awful food I ever heard of. She deserves a special place in Heaven for "Capt. D's" and assorted meals.

Add to these our "electronic friends" - <u>Carol Cookerly</u>, Sharon's employer in Atlanta and <u>Peggy Zinberg</u> in Washington. Their support and caring will always be remembered. In Charlotte, David's physician, <u>Dr. Josh Sumake</u> and Sharon's counselor, <u>Dr. Linda Smith</u> are owed our debt of thanks.

During the years before David's illness, he and I spent a lot of time together - separately and apart. We traveled to Lanai, Hawaii and to Jamaica and a number of places elsewhere in the US. To give you an idea of our relationship, let me give you a few examples.

David and I did many things together - usually quietly (to give you Sharon's and Peggy's perspective, "They must bore each other to death.") . Neither of us felt the need to talk as much as they. The two of us played golf (he much better than I), and we boated, fished and enjoyed our lake house at Lake Lure, NC. We especially enjoyed trout fishing in the streams and small rivers near our place. You will note I said "fishing", not "catching". At any rate, it was outdoors and fun. Two stories: We were trout fishing near a covered bridge - I casting in all of my Orvis regalia (most of it given to me by David and Sharon) when a car pulled up, and its occupants began taking many pictures of me and the bridge. When we got home, Peggy and Sharon heard the story and asked David, "Why did they take all of those pictures?" David quietly answered, "They had never seen one person wearing everything Orvis made." As to golf, he referred to me as "the most uninhibited golfer he had ever seen."

Shortly before David's illness - he was perhaps in his mid 30's then - we were fishing in a small stream well up in the NC mountains, near a row of houses. It became apparent that a house party was being held in one by a sorority from Clemson. Eager to say hello, David asked one of the young women about Clemson - only to be answered with "Sir"! I think it was the first time he had that term applied to himself - a good comeuppance.

Likewise, David and Peggy had a wonderful relationship. Having lost both of his parents a few years before, he was hungry for a family relationship. Peggy had gone to a "spouses' lecture" at one of my meetings, on "Your Identity". She later called Sharon and David, stating "I have no identity."

David promptly piped up with "Tell her she's a goddess mother-in-law." Peggy was assuaged.

However, long before this happened, when Sharon and David were first engaged, the teasing started. Peggy asked David, while preparing the wedding announcement, if he would mind if she included "the groom graduated from a large Southeastern university" rather than Clemson University. As a University of Georgia graduate, she had a deep-seated antipathy for Clemson. David quietly replied that his father always told him, "If you drive through Athens, Georgia, drive fast. If you go slow they throw a diploma in the car."

Their relationship was amazingly warm - he spent years buying Peggy presents - buying them himself. The last was less than 6 months before his death - a print by Picasso of a dachshund (we have 2) which proudly hangs in our home today.

A number of others must be noted. <u>Cam and Jamie Donovan and their children Samantha (5) and Ann (2)</u> especially. Sharon and Cam were room mates at Queens here in Charlotte. All four of you cared for Sharon and David in ways too numerous to count. We could never have made it without you. To <u>Chris and Robert Stowe</u>, the same comments. You all made their home a place of joy - not sadness. I will always recall David sitting in his power chair with a party swirling about him - and including him. Thank you all. To <u>Sheila and Bob Breitwiser</u>, for all of those trips from Spartanburg and your love and caring - thank you also. <u>To our son, Chuck, and his wife, Ann and children, Charlie, Katie and Oliver</u> - thanks for your trips from Iowa (Cedar Rapids, no less), your calls, e-mails and from the kids - texts, plus your taking care of Sharon in those times she came to you for rest and restoration - thank you very much (plus your helping to move them from Greenville to Charlotte).

A few others to thank – <u>Dr. Jeff and Nancy Giguere</u> - Sharon's oncologist in Greenville and the reason she is here today. <u>Rev. Joe Harvard</u>, our minister in Durham and the person who married Sharon and David - and who came here to hold this service. He and his wife, <u>Carlisle</u>, are our dear friends. <u>Judy Perrell and her family.</u> She was the realtor who found their home here - and grew to become a very dear friend of us all. <u>Menge Crawford</u>, who sang today - a new friend who has become very close to us all. Finally, to all of our <u>other friends and to neighbors and friends</u> in Charlotte - who belie the feeling that "people are distant". Thank you for your friendship and love to our children.

Let me close with a brief summary of a long and very difficult saga - a story of loss (too soon) and pain - of sadness, and despite the loss - of joy. Joy that David was with us for a short while, but a short while we will never forget.

On the evening of David's death, Cam, Jamie and their children, Sam and Ann, drove over to be with Sharon at her home. Cam told them that David had "died and gone to Heaven." Samantha (Sam), who is 5, asked her what that meant. Cam told her it meant he would be with Jesus, and that David would be able to walk and run and be whole again. In the wisdom of children, Sam added to her parents, "I am sure he will be able to talk again." Samantha - we all surely hope so.

Malvern King, a lawyer in Durham and a member of our church there, lost his father to ALS, and he has been a constant friend to us all. After his father's death, the elders of his church had a verse from Isaiah placed on a plaque and given to Mal. He in turn sent it to Sharon and David several months ago, as a statement particularly poignant for someone with ALS:

Isaiah Chapter 40, verse 31:

> "They who wait for the Lord shall renew their strength.
>
> They shall mount up with wings like eagles.
>
> They shall run and not be weary.
>
> They shall walk and not faint."

May David and Sharon, and all of us, now find peace and in all of our own ways, find new life after death.

Amen

Chapter Thirty-Two

Sharon slowly regained her strength and energy after David's death and memorial service. We spent time together in Charlotte and a week at Kiawah Island, joined by Chuck, Ann and their kids. This seemed to lift Sharon's spirits considerably. By September 2008 she had set out to decide what further direction she should pursue – for work, but more importantly, for fulfillment. We had little doubt what her direction would be – writing.

During David's illness Sharon had taken several classes in creative writing - one by the Charlotte Writers Club and another at Queens University, taught by Gilda Syverson who continued thereafter to help edit her work during this time (and you have read it in her first 28 chapters). She then made her application to Queens University for their Masters of Fine Arts, Creative Writing program for enrollment in the late spring of 2009. She later received a phone call from Dr. Fred Leebron, the Program Director, who was still working during his sabbatical in Barcelona, Spain, offering her admission to the program. His acceptance evaluation was a delight for Sharon: "Admit. This is powerful writing in all its moods – candid, funny, disbelieving, heartbroken – with a strong sense of the narrator's presence on the page. This narrator grabs the reader to tell a story, and it is definitely a story worth reading. Maybe one of its essential charms is the writer's self awareness, the quiet knowledge that underlies the lively telling. A definite admit." With admission accomplished Sharon headed into the new year with excitement for the future. Unfortunately, her story was soon to be frustrated. I have attached from her application her statement of purpose and two letters of recommendation.

Statement of Purpose

Sharon H. McAlister

In examining my motivations to enter the Queens MFA program I just had to take a look back at the past seven years. I am soon to be 49 years old and have gone through a fairly dramatic transformation during that time. At age 42 I was diagnosed with Stage 3 breast cancer and went through a very vigorous course of treatment that included an elective bilateral mastectomy, eight rounds of "dose-dense" chemotherapy (translation – horrid) and weeks of intense radiation. I never asked "why me?" I asked "why not me"?

I got through it, no worse for the wear, and stronger in myriad ways than I had ever anticipated. Within a month of the end of my treatment, my husband of 15 years was diagnosed with Amyotrophic Lateral Sclerosis (ALS) or Lou Gehrig's disease. I did ask "why him" on that one. For the uninitiated, the clinical description of ALS explains that nerve cells that control muscle cells are gradually lost. As these motor neurons are lost, the muscles they control become weak and then nonfunctional. Eventually, the person with ALS is paralyzed and dies. It's like watching a long, slow train wreck. He lost his battle seven months ago. I miss him.

I include this background not for sympathy or shock value, but to illustrate how I reached this juncture in my life and career. During David's illness I found that I was writing a memoir of this time in our lives. Only I was writing it in my head, which actually gets exhausting. When I happened upon a class, specifically geared to writing a memoir, it was the push I needed to actually put this story into words - on actual paper. They say that sometimes God whispers to you and sometimes he slaps you in the head. The opportunity to take this class was like a sledge hammer to my head. My story began spilling out of me – gushing if you please – and the joy and therapy the class provided was like a healing balm.

While my professional life has always included writing – many years of experience in public relations, a five-year stint as a contributing writer at *Greenville Magazine* and various other jobs that utilized my writing skills – I had always approached the assignments from a much more clinical and detached perspective. I interviewed people and researched the facts and was thorough in my work. Writing from a personal viewpoint was a whole new ballgame. I now had to interview myself. Not always easy or comfortable, but incredibly rewarding.

I am a highly self-directed person. I have worked for myself for the past several years, even on a part-time basis while caring for my husband. That is one of the reasons the low residency MFA program at Queens is appealing. There's nothing I like better than a self-imposed deadline. And in deciding to apply for this program I also considered my desire to continue learning about the craft of writing, the value of a healthy critique and the motivation of a nurturing and instructive environment.

The bottom line is that both my personal and professional goals are in alignment for probably the first time in my life. I have the tenacity and the curiosity to pursue this goal and look forward to the challenges that this program could bring to my life. I also think that my life experience has given me an entirely new sense of empathy, compassion and realism that will enhance my contribution to the program.

February 10, 2009
Office of Admissions
Master of Fine Arts Program
Queens University of Charlotte
1900 Selwyn Avenue
Charlotte, NC 28274

RE: Sharon Hammond McAlister

Dear Members of the Admissions Committee:

It is both an honor and privilege for me to submit this letter of recommendation for Sharon H. McAlister as a candidate for admission to the Master of Fine Arts Program at Queens University of Charlotte.

Through the many education positions I have held over the years (including principal, superintendent and most recently, President of the SC School for the Deaf and the Blind), I became acquainted with many impressive students – individuals whom I have found to be motivated, bright and hard-working. With these contacts and years of experience, I believe I have developed the ability to identify the characteristics that predict future success in their chosen academic fields. Thus, as a person who is well acquainted with Sharon McAlister, I am fully confident that she is exactly the type of individual who will be successful academically and in all other contexts of the Master of Fine Arts in Creative Writing Program at Queens University.

In serving as a reference for Ms. McAlister, I will comment on three key factors that should serve as strong measures of her interest and potential success in this creative program.

1. Her career experience in public relations relates well to the technical skills and challenging aspects of creative writing that enable her to present well a wide-ranging gamut of stories, topics and issues.

2. Her passion for writing will motivate her well as she explores ways to share stories and ideas with various audiences.

3. Her life experiences have molded her with strength and increased her ability to connect with other people through empathetic understanding.

It seems, to me that these three factors set Ms. McAlister apart from other candidates – even those who also are creatively and academically talented.

Ms. McAlister has shared with me that one of her primary goals is to complete successfully the MFA Creative Writing Program – a goal which is truly achievable for her if she is given the opportunity. She definitely has the potential (and also the determination) to be an exemplary student and a great asset to this program and to Queens University. As I reflect on Ms. McAlister's future, I see an individual who, if selected for the MFA Creative Writing Program, will bring great skills and passion to her studies and her future professional work in the creative writing field.

Thank you for your consideration of my letter of recommendation on the behalf of Sharon H, McAlister. I hope you will contact me if I can provide any further information about this letter or her candidacy for selection to this prestigious program.

Sincerely,

Sheila S. Breitweiser, Ed.D.
SRHS Foundation VP/Executive Director

Dear Members of the Admissions Committee:

Sharon McAlister has asked me for a letter of recommendation to accompany her application for the Master of Fine Arts in Creative Writing program, and I am happy to recommend her without reservation.

Sharon worked as a vice president for my company, Cookerly Public Relations, during the 1990's and I have continued to be associated with her both as a colleague and a friend ever since. She is intelligent, sharp-minded, a fast learner, and above all, an extremely talented writer. She is equally adept at translating complex topics into writing that is easy to understand as she is at adapting simple ideas into meaningful messages for different audiences. I have found her writing to be distinguished not only by her eloquence, but also by her creativity – which is never lacking.

I believe Sharon is not only well suited to benefit immensely from your Creative Writing program but will prove to be an exemplary student. Inasmuch as she will be proud to study in your Master of Fine Arts Program, I believe you will also be proud to count her among your graduates.

In closing, let me reiterate my recommendation of Sharon. If I might provide you with any additional information about this outstanding candidate, please do not hesitate to contact me.

Sincerely,

Carol Cookerly
President, Cookerly Public Relations
Atlanta, Georgia

Chapter Thirty-Three

January 2009 saw a heavy snow fall on North Carolina (at least, heavy for us). Sharon's outdoor umbrella fell over, and she attempted to re-erect it herself. Midway through lifting it, she developed acute, severe low back pain. She tried heat, rest and analgesics for a week or so with little improvement. She saw her physicians who obtained an x-ray of her spine and then an MRI study. The findings showed extensive spread of breast cancer in her lower spine, with partial collapse of some areas (accounting for her acute pain). Next came other scans and tests, and it appeared a number of other sites were involved. It was obvious that cure would be very unlikely, so Sharon made the decision to obtain local x-ray therapy to attempt to improve her pain and to adjust her antitumor medications in an attempt to slow/stop the tumor's progression. During this time she again remained in Charlotte in her home and Peggy and I spent considerable time there. Felicia resumed her role as caregiver.

Believe it or not, one night during this time someone broke into her home and stole her computer, purse and some jewelry – all while she was asleep in the house. I hope there is a special, hot place for that individual in the future. Fortunately, she was not injured.

Regretfully, Sharon asked for and was granted a delay in entering the MFA program at Queens, but looked hopefully to a remission from her disease and later entry into the program. However, while her back pain was improved (she later even made another trip to Chuck's home in Iowa), the disease did not stop its progression. We offered repeatedly to bring her to Duke/Durham, but she wanted to stay in Charlotte and to receive her therapy there. At this stage I could not argue with her.

Throughout the last years of David's life and continuing after his death Sharon had served as a neighbor, friend and counselor to two early teenaged boys who lived on either side of her home – John and Michael. This continued until her death. They came singly and together, bringing problems they were struggling with for her advice. They usually sat out back on the patio and Sharon, who "told it like it was", offered advice and help. Both were from divided homes; one was acting out, the other living with one parent. Both were great kids. I was amazed how close each had become to Sharon and how much they respected her – as did their parents. I was also impressed at how much they did for Sharon and David with the yard or the dogs, especially when first, David, and then, Sharon, could not do them. Additionally, one of the mothers, Jane Grayson, became a wonderful friend of Sharon and a "can do" person for many of her needs.

Letters came to us from each of the boys shortly after Sharon's death. John wrote from an essay he gave orally at the end of his school year - in a course about what makes for "Life Long Success". He told (the whole middle school) the story of his relationship with Sharon. He described how she listened with a young heart, but gave counsel based on better experience. He described how she could make him see things more clearly... He told them how strong she had been during David's long illness, then death. Then, he told them that Sharon passed away suddenly just a few weeks before and that he would miss her forever. He ended his story by saying that according to a poem,

> "to know that one life has breathed easier because you have lived, is to have succeeded."

John went on after this to say "I know that I have breathed easier because Sharon lived, and I also believe that she breathed easier, knowing me." What an amazing tribute!

Michael wrote:

"To Sharon's Parents:

I want you to know that I'm so sorry about Sharon's death. I want you to know that Sharon was like family and someone who I could go to and talk to if I had a problem. She will <u>always</u> be in my thoughts, my heart and prayers... My favorite times were when John, Jane, me and Sharon would be on the deck and we all would talk and share our thoughts. ...I am going to miss her so much.

I'm always going to be here if you need me.

MS"

Chapter Thirty-Four

In early May of 2009 Sharon called and asked if I would come down and bring her back to Durham and I perceived she was near the end of her ability to fight the disease. I went down, gathered all of her medical needs, loaded Sharon and her two Jack Russells into my car and returned to Durham on what was likely the most difficult trip I would ever make. Sharon was asleep in the front seat, braced by pillows, and the dogs were roaming the back seat, repeatedly letting the window down and barking (I had no cage). I was even stopped by the Highway Patrol for speeding, but the trooper was forgiving when he saw my predicament and let me go on with just a warning. Sharon spent several days at our home and then entered Duke Hospital for a re-evaluation of her disease. It became rapidly apparent that it had continued to spread and expand. Brain, liver and lungs were now involved, in addition to many new bony structures. There was very little hope that even with the most vigorous (and taxing) efforts the disease could be cured, or even slowed down with such difficult therapies. After considering her options, Sharon elected no further treatment, but only symptomatic (palliative) care and was moved to the new Duke Hospice in Durham.

One day while Sharon was hospitalized at Duke she was drinking a Coke, holding the can while she sipped. As she was falling asleep, her mom who was with her noted she was about to drop the can. Peggy reached to take the can when Sharon woke fully and pulled the can back – "No, Mom, I want to control it." I guess that simply shows how tough she really was.

Sharon knew fully that she would likely never leave the hospice. It was truly a haven, staffed by wonderfully caring and competent individuals. While she was there – a couple of stories.

For likely the first time for a person in such a facility, Sharon wanted a haircut, so Peggy called her hairdresser, Pam. Pam came in the next several hours and shampooed and cut her hair. Sharon also decided she needed some "Crocs" shoes. She said, "It would be nice to have them to go out onto the patio (in Charlotte) to water the plants." Do you have any doubt that we got the "Crocs" two hours later and she wore them in her room.

Chuck came from Iowa for two days and spent very good and meaningful time with her and with us. They even ordered two pizzas one night and ate most of them. We all spent most of the time with her until she died peacefully on May 28, 2009, after ten days at the hospice.

Early that morning I was sitting on our deck when an owl settled in the tree beside me – we had never before had one in our yard. En route to the hospice shortly after I had seen the owl, I received a call from them that Sharon had died shortly before. The owl has continued to be seen at intervals ever since. Just coincidence???

———————

I have attached an e-mail from Dr. Leebron, the Program Director of the MFA Program at Queens. He sent it to us regarding comments he made about Sharon as part of his closing address to graduates of the program on May 30, 2009:

"Betty, Mike, Melissa, fellow faculty, fellow MFAs, students, writers, friends, and most important, new graduates:

Last night, when I returned to the dorm, I found a message waiting for me from the brother of a writer we had admitted for this May, a woman who had been unable to join us due to the recurrence of a horrific illness. He wrote: "I wanted to let you know that Sharon passed away yesterday. I want to reiterate just how much our conversation and your emails helped comfort her."

At first, I was struck by the incredible generosity of this e-mail from Chuck, that so soon he had found the time and the energy to write to me. I really marveled at that, as I have been that brother, too; and I instantly felt quite certainly from all I had seen and heard this week from all of you, that in one form or another all of you have been that brother, too. I think it is one of the joys and the privileges of working in a low-residency program, that one gets the sense of a real wealth and depth of experience from everyone here, that one gets the sense of everyone's mutually earned humanity. Then, as I began to wrestle with this, I could not help thinking about all the things Sharon would miss here. I thought of how she would miss getting to know people like you, people who are good at listening and good at talking, good at sharing stories and good at offering help to one another, good at having fun and good at knowing when to stop, and so good at writing. I thought of how we would miss getting to know her, and how we would miss getting to be a part of that transformation for her that you've all experienced here, that essential progression from uncertainty to confidence, that essential evolution of a concrete and durable relationship with the people who work here and learn here in service of this program, and that feeling that you can count on us for what you need to further yourself as a writer. And then it occurred to me that somehow, in Sharon's too brief interaction with us, that some of this had already managed to happen, that in the brevity of our exchange of phone calls and e-mails, in our two months of mutual anticipation of her arrival here, she had managed to get the essence of us. "Your program and her writing were incredibly important to her up to the very end," Chuck wrote last night, and I feel like I know in part something of what he meant. I have gotten to know it from listening to you all this week.

I can't help thinking of Sharon and how much it would have meant to her and to us to one day be here like you, but I can recognize that at least as a program we were able to let her know how proud of her we already were. And I am so glad and so lucky to have the opportunity today to tell you how proud we are of you, and , really, how proud we have always been of you. You have honored us with your presence, you have accepted our challenge, and we do not doubt that you will fulfill your promise.

You, you thirty-two, are indeed Masters of Fine Arts.

Thank you and congratulations."

On June 6, 2009 we held Sharon's memorial service at our church in Durham, NC. Here Sharon was baptized, grew up and was married. The church was filled, and once again the Reverend Joe Harvard provided a moving homily to Sharon. Dr. Sheila Breitweiser provided an often humorous but frequently sad assessment of Sharon's life to help all know who she was. I have attached their words. The music was beautiful. I did not speak that day as I knew I would simply break up. Sheila and Joe (whose homily was entitled "A Light in the Darkness") did masterful jobs for Sharon and for us.

Again, after the service we held a reception at our home – many attended and many stayed late. Margaret Scearce, our long-time caterer, now retired, returned with all of her family to provide the food and drink. This too was like David's – a wake – a celebration of life.

David and Sharon are now in the same place, and their ashes were buried together in the Memorial Garden at First Presbyterian Church on Main Street in Durham. We visit often as it is adjacent to our church. A reminder of two wonderful young people who suffered and then were freed – and truly joined forever.

Reflections On A Special Life

Sharon Hammond McAlister
Memorial Service: Saturday, June 6, 2009
First Presbyterian Church, Durham, NC
Sheila Breitweiser, EdD

To Sharon's devoted family and friends (and especially Peggy and Charlie and Chuck and Ann, Charlie, Katie and Oliver),

On behalf of Bob and me, thank you for the opportunity today to share some memories of Sharon and what she means to all of us.

To Reverend Joe Harvard, I offer my apologies. For after years of telling you that you missed obvious exit points during your sermons, I must confess that I have no clear exit strategy today – just an array of Sharon stories that will remind us all of just how special she was. So let me begin my comments about the person of this amazing woman and her life.

There is a poem that many of you may have heard that describes the essence of a person's life as the dash that we place between their years of birth and death. The short version of the poem is to say that it's not the number of years a person lives, but what happens in their lives in those years. You get it now … the "dash" represents the life we live between our birth and death.

Personally, I have found this poem to be rather corny – and I suspect that Sharon Hammond McAlister is looking down on us right now, hand on her hip (can't you just see her?!), and ready to have a few choice words for me about daring to embarrass her with this sappy stuff about her life. But, I must admit to you as I think about Sharon, and her life, and all that she meant to our group gathered here today … the dash idea really catches my heart and mind.

For Sharon surely did not have the pleasure of living a long life, but, oh my, what a life she managed to pack into the all too brief time we had her here with us. My hope today is to share some memories with you about Sharon's life so that we can celebrate the time we had her and remember her for the beautiful, brave, funny and fantastic wife, daughter, sister, aunt and friend that she was to all of us. And, if somehow we miss out on the joy of her incredibly wicked sense of humor as we remember her, I am absolutely convinced that she will personally hold me accountable for this when I see her again some day.

We first met Sharon over 40 years ago when she was a beautiful little girl with blond hair, a scattering of freckles across her nose and a great sense of humor that was far beyond her years. Funny, but that is the way we will always remember Sharon from the last time we saw her … except that she was a beautiful willowy woman with blond hair and still a few freckles – and the sense of humor that, like good wine, had aged well over the years.

What happened in the years between is the stuff that books are written about – which was exactly what Sharon had planned to do when she was accepted to the Masters of Fine Arts Creative Writing Program at Queens University in Charlotte. Sharon's writing sample for them was taken from a journal she was writing to chronicle the experiences that she and the love of her life, David, had undergone during his lengthy battle with ALS (Lou Gehrig's Disease). The head of the creative writing program was so wowed by her writing that he called Sharon from Europe to let her know of her acceptance to the program. When Sharon called us that day to share her news, she was more excited than I could ever remember. All I could think was, "Leave it to Sharon to take the painful experiences of David's and her illnesses and turn them into something inspiring and beautiful." She just never gave up on believing that we can find something good in every life experience, even the sacrifices and sadness she experienced in caring for David during the last years of his life. Who knows? If she had been granted the time to finish writing her book (which, in typical Sharon fashion, she had entitled "Lucky Girl"), it might have been made into a movie and Sharon and David's love story might have been immortalized by the likes of Jennifer Aniston and Brad Pitt in their reunion film. (Now, I am truly certain that Sharon is going to have a serious reprimand for me when we meet again: "Really, Sheila, Jennifer and Brad?")

But there really was something magical about the story Sharon was planning to write through her highly anticipated enrollment in the Creative Writing Program. Just in recent days Peggy shared with Bob and me an incredible exchange of e-mails that took place between Sharon's brother Chuck and the director of the Creative Writing Program. In her relatively brief contact time with the director, Sharon had so impressed him and touched his heart that he spoke eloquently of her in his commencement remarks to the 2009 graduating class of the Creative Writing Program. In addition, Chuck was even contacted by a member of Sharon's incoming class who described how much Sharon's writing group would miss her and her creative talents. Along with those contacts, Peggy and Charlie just heard from one of her new friends in a Charlotte writing group to say that Sharon will be greatly missed (and I quote) "for her wit, her sweet Southern accent and her pure honest heart."

Isn't it amazing the degree of impact Sharon has had on so many lives – those of us who knew and loved her for many years, those who knew her for too short a time and those who only knew of her even though they never had the joy of a personal relationship with Sharon?

Along with our knowing and loving Sharon for more than 40 years, it should be very obvious that her parents (Peggy and Charlie) and her brother Chuck and sister-in-law Ann have all been near and dear to the hearts of so many of us. Their family brings to mind some old country expressions that we can quote directly from Peggy's parents (Daddy Bill and Mother Irene) like "The apple doesn't fall far from the tree," and "The chip doesn't fall far from the block." Sharon's indomitable spirit could also be described as stubborn, pig-headed, determined, pragmatic and other similar adjectives. Sharon came by this naturally since Peggy and Charlie personify the immovable object and the unstoppable force. Let's face it ... being determined, bossy and in control was in Sharon's DNA. Sharon had these wonderful expressions that reflected her determination to deal with whatever life threw her way – expressions like "Put on your big girl panties and deal with it" (especially effective when she was chastising any female family members or friends who might be falling victim to a big dose of self pity). Or, her way of saying "Ya think"? – particularly in response to really dumb remarks by physicians (sorry, Charlie!) like "David might be a little depressed about his deteriorating health." When it came to such practical matters as life and death, Sharon possessed grace, wisdom and practical sense not only beyond her years, but in reality far beyond what any of us will ever know.

Now, don't think for a minute that Sharon ever lost that wry sense of humor that was her trademark from her youthful days. She always had a special ability to make you laugh and to surprise you with her comments. During her high school days Sharon spent one Thanksgiving with our family. When we began working on the menu for our holiday meal, Sharon just shouted out, "Katie, bar the door." Being much more of a Yankee then than I am now, I was afraid someone named Katie was trying to break into our house – until Sharon helpfully explained that this was a phrase describing her excitement over the good meal ahead. While Sharon got us again many times with her quick wit, one of the most memorable was the day of her wedding to David. Bob and I were so honored to be asked to be the greeters at the reception – welcoming guests before the arrival of the bridal party. In trying to be the perfect hostess I sat the first guests down and regaled them with food, drink and my personal best attention. After all, it was a bunch of guys who were clearly David's college friends. The only problem was that Bob had to alert me to the fact that I was entertaining the band (instead of letting them entertain the guests). When he told Sharon about my social blunder, she had the brightest twinkle in her eye and joyfully reminded me (for decades) about inviting the band to sit, drink, and wait for the arrival of the bride and groom.

Sharon's sense of humor was truly contagious. On many occasions I would stop by Peggy and Charlie's home when she and David and Chuck and Ann would all be there. The happiness they projected would blanket the house in light and laughter as everyone joined in whatever teasing and fun were being exchanged by the two young couples. Sharon's ability to blend hope with mounds of humor was so clearly evident whenever you were with her. Bob and I would always plan our visits with Sharon as opportunities to check on her and lift her spirits. Thus, we were continuously amazed when, at the end of each visit, we'd leave with the realization that the gifts of hope and laughter had been extended to us by Sharon – and not the other way around.

Still, Sharon's softer side was always there to help others. One Christmas (during David's time of illness), someone told her about a little boy whose mom told him there would be no Christmas at their house. Upon hearing this troubling news, Sharon was immediately transformed into a woman on a mission to ensure that this child would have a Christmas – and not with just a few toys and books. Sharon gave out assignments for gift selections (beginning, of course, with Peggy and Charlie) until an entire list of gifts has been purchased, wrapped and delivered for the little guy on Christmas Eve. Sharon considered it "Mission Accomplished" when all the gifts were opened and the little boy announced it was the best Christmas he ever had.

Sharon's never-give-up spirit was never more evident than during these last months of her life. She knew what was ahead for her, after all, she had already traveled once down this road with David during the years she cared for him. But, even facing death for a second time, Sharon never gave up her fight. When she arrived at Peggy and Charlie's for her last trip, she told her mother that she wished she had a pair of "Crocs" (those brightly colored plastic outdoor shoes) – which she noted would be very good to have when she got back home and needed to water her plants. Needless to say, she soon had a pair of Crocs that she wore whenever she needed shoes until the day she died. You won't be surprised to know that anything she even mentioned wanting was immediately delivered by either Peggy or Charlie – and, as Peggy told us, "Lucky for us that Sharon never mentioned wanting or needing a Rolls Royce."

For those of you who knew Sharon during her battle with cancer, you will recall also that she still always managed to look great. She had such style that she even managed to make a baseball cap and an artificial pony tail look terrific. Sharon would be the first to admit that vanity did play a role in her efforts – especially when it came to her lovely hair. She had her own way of describing hair dye. Sharon never "colored" or "dyed" her hair, rather she simply "restored it to its natural color". And it shouldn't surprise you to know that one of her last requests was to have a special hair cut. Of course, Peggy managed to grant that wish through a sweet friend named Pam who arrived at Hospice in no time flat to wash and cut Sharon's hair.

These memories are just a flavor of the amazing life Sharon Hammond McAlister brought to this world. But rather than referencing the "dash" in the poem, there is a modified passage from Proverbs that, to me, perfectly describes this amazing woman: "A woman of valor, who can find her? She stretches out her hand to the needy. Strength and honor are her garments; she shall rejoice in the time to come. She is honored for her kindness and generosity. She speaks words of wisdom. Compassion is her virtue. She is devoted to her family. Give her the fruits of her toil, and she will be praised in the gates for her deeds."

Maybe even better suited to Sharon's personality (and her love of light and brightness), we might reflect on this old campfire song that she and Chuck probably sang years ago when they were kids attending Camp Thunderbird on Lake Wylie, South Carolina: "This little light of mine, I'm going to let it shine. This little light of mine, I'm going to let it shine. Let it shine, let it shine, let it shine."

Sharon, I hope you'll forgive us (especially me) for all this sentimental stuff today as we rejoiced for your life and light among us. We thank you for your tolerance of our shared stories of how you made us laugh and cry. Most of all, we want you to know how much we love and miss you – and that the book you had planned to write about a lucky girl is already printed in our hearts and minds, never to be forgotten by your loving family and friends.

Epilogue

Not much more to say. Three weeks after Sharon's memorial service, Chuck and Ann joined us for one last time in Charlotte to close Sharon and David's home. Chuck had arranged for "pods" to be delivered and a dumpster, and we spent three days going through every nook and cranny. Throwing away everything not needed or wanted by us, moving some furniture and valuables out along with packing up clothes and items we felt were recyclable and leaving many things out that others may want. We asked 8-10 individuals to come by at a set time to take (or mark for later pick-up) items that they might want to keep (furniture, others) and by the end of the time we were left with only a bit. We asked Felicia to get rid of the rest and have Goodwill pick up the recyclables we did not want. As expected, those were days of a person laughing in one room while another was crying elsewhere. We had kept the sofa and stuffed chairs in their family room separate for another use. One evening during this time their neighbors held a "cook out" for us and remembered Sharon and David. What wonderful folks. Once again, it was sad but happy for us all. We listed the house for sale (another story), loaded up the "pods" and returned to our homes. I do not envy Chuck and Ann whenever they have to do the same with our home, and I assure the reader I do <u>not</u> plan to do theirs.

Now, the remaining sofa and chairs. Jane Grayson, the neighbor next door, knew of a new, experimental theater opening shortly that needed such furniture. The audience were to be seated on living room furniture at a venue for writers. Wouldn't Sharon be pleased to know her furniture was a part of this?. They took the items and used them when they opened. Included was a reading of "David's Day" in remembrance. It is my understanding they are in regular use at the theater to this day, a key contribution to this new writers/theater venue.

Sharon and David had no children. Their will left their entire estate to Chuck and Ann's three children – Charlie, Katie and Oliver – for their educations. All of their funds were ultimately transferred to accounts in their names and their college (and any other advanced degrees) are assured. Charlie was just admitted to Northwestern University for this fall. They should be able to attend any school they wish (and can be accepted to). We all (ourselves and Chuck and Ann) are left with the memories of two wonderful individuals for whom we rejoice and mourn as we move forward. Their dogs came to live with us (four dogs – two Jack Russells and our two long-haired dachshunds – it's not all peace and quiet).

We later found a blog (see, I can be a part of the "new generation") by Anne Lynn, a woman who had Stage 4 lung cancer and who was in the class at Queens that Sharon had attended:

"Wednesday, June 3, 2009

~51~ Lucky Girl!

Today I was going to give ideas on how you might be able to help someone while in the chemo room. But after receiving a phone call from Gilda, my writing teacher at Queens University, I found it imperative I share about Sharon. Gilda called to give me the sad news that Sharon, a friend from our class, had passed away. I was flushed with grief listening, hardly grasping that she meant our sweet Sharon. In January 2008 I was fortunate to have met Sharon. She was an excellent writer who wrote with compassion, honesty, zest and understandably a bit of sarcasm. Her stories included the battles she endured while living with breast cancer. She began reading us different chapters from her future book. They were not always in order so our group did not know some of the story until the following fall. When class picked up again after the summer Sharon's tone switched from heavy to light. But the premises of her chapters consisted of a mixture of hope and mounds of humor. What we did not know till then was that along with her own battle of breast cancer she took care of her husband, David, who was battling ALS. ALS, also known as Lou Gehrig's disease, is a progressive neurodegenerative disease that affects nerve cells in the brain and the spinal cord which eventually leads to death. Sadly, David had passed away over the summer. As Gilda finished telling me about

Sharon the same sad feelings flashed through me as when Sharon had read her chapter about David dying. As I listened to Gilda, I thought back on how Sharon wrote fondly of her love for David, her caring parents and the fact that her dad was a doctor. Unfortunately, I know firsthand cancer doesn't care who it picks and kills. Anyone's a target. As I stayed on the phone with Gilda we concurred that we were the lucky ones to have been able to meet Sharon. We will greatly miss her wit, her southern sweet accent along with her pure honest heart. Sharon left us with hope. Hope for the day. Hope that you can move past pain. Hope that you can move through the death of a dear loved one like her David. Hope to believe there's a place for her new day now spent with David in a life empty from all diseases, filled with only love. If I remember correctly, the title to Sharon McAlister's book was "Lucky Girl".

I will close this book with two poems which mean a great deal to all of us. Sharon and David will live on in our hearts and minds, and I am quite sure for Chuck, Ann, Charlie, Katie and Oliver. What wonderful memories these are. Sharon's book might better be titled, "Lucky Family".

One teardrop

One teardrop
That is all
For some reason
I can't cry
Even though
It is sad
For some reason
I can't cry
I hope
You get better soon
Because I am
Going to cry

Oliver Hammond

April 14, 2009

On hearing of his aunt's recurrence
of breast cancer

First Born

The day you were born, I don't
Remember
If it was warm or not
If the sun shone
Or rain
Slashed across the sky
Obscured by pain and doubt
But I know
That I held you
For hours, stared at you
In awe –
And felt the warmth assault me.
Felt all the old, forgotten smiles
Creep back –
Until I wasn't sure
Which of us
Had just been born.

Leslie Garcia

Made in the USA
Lexington, KY
12 May 2012